The ADHD Handbook

The ADHD Handbook

A Handbook for Parents and Professionals
on Attention Deficit Hyperactivity Disorder

Alison Munden and Jon Arcelus

Jessica Kingsley Publishers
London and Philadelphia

The right of Alison Munden and Jon Arcelus to be identified as authors of this work has been asserted by them in accordance with the Copyright, Designs and Patents Act 1988.

First published in the United Kingdom in 1999 by
Jessica Kingsley Publishers Ltd,
116 Pentonville Road,
London N1 9JB,
England
and
325 Chestnut Street,
Philadelphia, PA 19106, USA.
www.jkp.com

Library of Congress Cataloging in Publication Data
A CIP catalog record for this book is available from the Library of Congress

British Library Cataloguing in Publication Data
Munden, Alison
The ADHD handbook : a guide for parents and professionals
1.Attention-deficit hyperactivity disorder – Great Britain – Popular works
I.Title II.Arcelus, Jon
618.9'28589

ISBN 1 85302 756 1

Printed and Bound in Great Britain by
Athenaeum Press, Gateshead, Tyne and Wear

To our parents

Contents

Acknowledgements

We are grateful to the children and families we have had the pleasure to work with and who have taught us so much.

We would also like to thank the following people:

Andrea Bilbow for introducing us to so many ideas and people and for her ongoing work with the family support groups promoting a wider awareness and understanding of ADHD in the UK.

Dr Colin Tinline, Dr Linda Winkley and Dr Sumi Handy for providing the opportunity, encouragement and support that made this book possible.

Dr Walter Bouman, Dr Jeff Munden and Jill Munden for reviewing this manuscript and for their useful and constructive comments.

Finally, we would like to thank to our publisher Jessica Kingsley and her team for making this book happen.

Preface

Historically, a number of terms have been used to describe the disorder presenting with symptoms of ADHD. These include Minimal Brain Dysfunction or Damage (MBD), Hyperkinetic Reaction, and Hyperkinesis. Throughout this book we refer to it as Attention Deficit Hyperactivity Disorder, or ADHD. Attention Deficit Hyperactivity Disorder is sometimes also called ADD (Attention Deficit Disorder). The two terms are often used synonymously: strictly speaking, they refer to different, although very similar, probably related conditions. People with ADHD have difficulties with attention span, and are impulsive and hyperactive. Those with ADD do not have hyperactivity but share the problems associated with impulsiveness and attention deficit. In both cases the symptoms are present to a degree that is abnormal for the age and intellectual ability of the person. Some doctors and professionals, particularly in Europe, refer to people with either sets of symptoms as having Hyperkinetic Disorder.

ADHD is a disorder with an underlying biological cause. It is not simply the end result of poor parenting, or an unpleasant and irritating disposition on the part of the child. In some ways it is similar to other illnesses that occur in children, in that it can have serious effects if it is not adequately treated.

ADHD is not a newly recognised condition. People with these symptoms have probably always existed. In 1902 a British physician, Frederic Still, described 'abnormal psychical conditions' in children and the concept of 'deficit in moral control'. He described, in the *Lancet*, a syndrome characterised by a deficit in sustained attention, neurological abnormalities including choreiform movements (twitching), minor congenital anomalies, restlessness, fidgetiness, aggression, rule breaking, and destructiveness. He attributed those symptoms to an organic (biological) and constitutional cause.

In 1937 Bradley described the unexpected effect of Amphetamine on hyperactivity and other behavioural problems in the *American Journal of Psychiatry*. By the 1960s and 1970s the diagnosis of ADHD and the prescription of Amphetamines had become a very common practice amongst paediatricians in the USA. In contrast, the diagnosis and treatment of these symptoms remained a rather rare event in Europe.

In the UK and France the dominant theories of children's psychiatric disorders stressed psychological causes, and this may have restricted diagnoses of hyperactivity, which would have implied physical cause and treatment.

During the 1970s and 1980s intensive scientific research and the development of explicit diagnostic criteria made ADHD the most written about and most cited childhood condition in the *Index Medicus* (the directory of medical research articles). As a result of this, ADHD is now recognised in Britain and in other countries in Europe as a disorder with an underlying biological cause that can be successfully treated.

Over the past five to ten years there has been an increasing awareness of this disorder in the UK, resulting in many more referrals to child psychiatrists and paediatricians.

Recent clinical experience and research has documented the continuation of symptoms into adulthood. Much more is known about ADHD as it presents in childhood and adolescence, than how it appears later in life. This book is written primarily with young people in mind, although much of its content is applicable to people of any age. The chapter 'ADHD in Adults' contains a synopsis of current knowledge and understanding pertaining to ADHD as it occurs in later life.

Prior to receiving a diagnosis and appropriate treatment, many families we have met in the ADHD clinics have felt a mounting sense of frustration and increasing despondency. Parents are usually the first to recognise that there is something seriously wrong with their child's behaviour. Many of their attempts to find either an explanation for this or a way of rectifying it have been unsuccessful. Hopelessness is a common feeling amongst the families of children with ADHD. They may, in addition, have been personally blamed for their child's difficulties and even accused of being 'bad parents'.

Once the underlying cause of their child's difficulties has been recognised and a diagnosis of ADHD has been made, parents may experience a huge sense of relief. At the same time it becomes apparent that there are many issues to be addressed, and effective solutions to be found. To prevent unnecessary teasing, bullying, or abuse of the patient's right to privacy and confidentiality regarding their condition and treatment, it is necessary to consider who needs to know what, how much they need to know and when they need to know it. These decisions should involve the patient, his or her parents if the patient is a child, and the professionals involved. In the case of childhood disorders, explaining the child's difficulties and treatment accurately and sensitively to other children in the family and to their classmates at school can be positive and helpful, enlisting the support of others, rather than encouraging ridicule and rejection.

When young people are diagnosed as having ADHD they themselves usually have many questions about the diagnosis: what is wrong, what can be done, and what is going to happen to them. Their families, teachers and friends also have questions to ask, as they need to understand what is going on in order to help.

In the case of children presenting with possible ADHD it is important that a careful assessment is done in order to make an accurate diagnosis and plan effective treatment. Many conditions present with some or all of the core symptoms of ADHD. It is essential to establish whether or not ADHD is present and if it is occurring at the same time as another disorder. A detailed account both of the disorders that could be involved, and of how the assessment is carried out, is described in the chapters that follow.

This book outlines what ADHD is, the symptoms and difficulties often associated with it, and the sort of treatments and interventions available. It is written from a specifically UK viewpoint and offers suggestions of where, or from whom more information and practical help can be found. We have attempted to present a concise, comprehensive and cohesive account of both theoretical and practical aspects of ADHD, in a form that is accessible to all interested professionals and parents. This book is also intended to act as a practical handbook, assisting parents and professionals attempting to understand and to help young people with ADHD, and to direct them to further sources of information and assistance. Much of the latter information is contained in the resources section at the end of the book.

Whilst writing this book we conducted a wide search of current scientific literature. We have drawn on our own clinical experience and that of senior and eminent colleagues practising both in the UK and in other countries.

We have attempted to include only information that is widely accepted to be accurate within conventional professional circles. We have tried to ensure that all the information, where possible, is based on evidence published in peer-reviewed international journals. In doing so we have tried to exclude any controversial or inaccurate advice, of which much abounds. Although written primarily for families and professionals living and working in the UK, the recommendations and advice contained within it are in line with those included in the 'Practice Parameters for the Assessment and Treatment of Children, Adolescents and Adults with Attention Deficit/Hyperactivity Disorder', published by the American Academy of Child and Adolescent Psychiatry (Dulcan October 1997). It is therefore appropriate for use in many countries.

Much of our own knowledge and understanding of ADHD comes not from books, scientific journals or other professional colleagues, but from our patients. We continue to learn from the experiences of the young people and families that we meet in our daily work as clinicians, and remain indebted to them for sharing their thoughts and experiences.

CHAPTER I

What is ADHD?

Doctors and other professionals who assess and treat people with physical or mental illnesses or other emotional or behavioural problems, try whenever possible to make a diagnosis.

The medical profession from all over the world continues to meet to refine a system of classifying syndromes, disorders and illnesses. As a result, names (diagnostic labels or 'diagnoses') are assigned to conditions that are recognised throughout the world's scientific and medical communities. The use of well-recognised classification systems ensures that any patient presenting anywhere in the world with a specific set of symptoms and clinical signs would be given the same diagnosis. This enables doctors and other professionals to use research that has already been carried out on patients with those symptoms, in order to:

1. Help them to predict the likely cause of the symptoms

2. Predict the course that the illness is likely to take

3. Decide on which treatment is likely to be most effective.

It is important during the assessment and treatment of any medical, psychiatric, emotional or behavioural disorder that the professionals involved are absolutely clear on what is 'wrong', or what the 'diagnosis' is. Having a diagnosis attached to their symptoms often enables the young person, adult, or their family to access certain sources of help. This could mean that they are able to receive effective medical treatment, to have additional or special provision of educational resources, receive extra benefits or be re-housed. In some cases these interventions may relieve or even cure the symptoms that led to the diagnosis being made in the first place.

The diagnostic criteria used by health professionals are constantly being up-dated and improved upon, as our understanding of illnesses and disorders increases. There are two classification systems (or sets of diagnostic criteria) currently in use:

1.   The classification system of the World Health Organisation (*The International Classification of Diseases, 10th edition,* or ICD-10).

2.   The classification system published by the American Psychiatric Association (*The Diagnostic and Statistical Manual of Mental Disorders, 4th edition,* or DSM-IV).

The diagnostic criteria are as follows:

ICD-10: Hyperkinetic Disorder	DSM-IV Attention Deficit Hyperactivity Disorder
	A. Either (1) or (2): *(1) Six or more of the following symptoms of inattention that have persisted for at least six months to a degree that is maladaptive and inconsistent with developmental level:*
Inattention	**Inattention**
At least six of the following symptoms of inattention have persisted for at least six months, to a degree that is maladaptive and inconsistent with the developmental level of the child:	(a) often fails to give close attention to details or makes careless mistakes in school work, work, or other activities (b) often has difficulty sustaining attention in tasks or play activities

(1) often fails to give close attention to details or makes careless errors in school work, work, or other activities

(2) often fails to sustain attention in tasks or play activities

(3) often appears not to listen to what is being said to him or her

(4) often fails to follow through on instructions or to finish homework, chores, or duties in the workplace (not because of oppositional behaviour or failure to understand instructions)

(5) is often impaired in organising tasks and activities

(6) often avoids tasks, like housework, that require sustained mental effort

(7) often loses things necessary for certain tasks or activities, such as school assignments, pencils, books, toys, or tools

(8) is often easily distracted by external stimuli

(9) is often forgetful in the course of daily activities

Hyperactivity

At least three of the following symptoms of hyperactivity have persisted for at least six months, to a degree that is maladaptive and inconsistent with the developmental level of the child:

(c) often does not seem to listen when spoken to directly

(d) often does not follow through on instructions and fails to finish school work, chores, or duties in the workplace (not due to oppositional behaviour or failure to understand instructions)

(e) often has difficulty organising tasks and activities

(f) often avoids, dislikes, or is reluctant to engage in tasks that require sustained mental effort (such as schoolwork or homework)

(g) often loses things necessary for tasks or activities (e.g. toys, school assignments, pencils, books or tools)

(h) is often easily distracted by extraneous stimuli

(i) is often forgetful in daily activities

(2) Six (or more) of the following symptoms of hyperactivity–impulsivity have persisted for at least six months to a degree that is maladaptive and inconsistent with developmental level:

Hyperactivity

(a) often fidgets with hands or feet or squirms in seat

(b) often leaves seat in classroom or in other situations in which remaining seated is expected

(1) often fidgets with hands or feet or squirms on seat

(2) leaves seat in classroom or in other situations in which remaining seated is expected

(3) often runs about or climbs excessively in situations in which it is inappropriate (in adolescents or adults, only feelings of restlessness may be present)

(4) is often unduly noisy in playing, or has difficulty in engaging quietly in leisure activities

(5) exhibits a persistent pattern of excessive motor activity that is not substantially modified by social context or demands.

(c) often runs about or climbs excessively in situations in which it is inappropriate (in adolescents or adults, may be limited to subjective feelings of restlessness)

(d) often has difficulty playing or engaging in leisure activities quietly

(e) is often 'on the go' or often acts 'as if driven by a motor'

(f) often talks excessively

Impulsivity

At least one of the following symptoms of impulsivity has persisted for at least six months, to a degree that is maladaptive and inconsistent with the developmental level of the child:

(1) often blurts out answers before the questions have been completed

(2) often fails to wait in lines or await turns in games or group situations

(3) often interrupts or intrudes on others (e.g. butts into others' conversations or games)

(4) often talks excessively without appropriate response to social restraints

Impulsivity

(g) often blurts out answers before questions have been completed

(h) often has difficulty awaiting turn

(i) often interrupts or intrudes on others (e.g. butts into conversations or games)

The differences between DSM-IV and ICD-10

Traditionally, psychiatrists in the UK have preferred to use the ICD-10 diagnostic criteria when making psychiatric diagnoses.

There are significant differences between the ICD-10 diagnostic criteria (the classification system published by the World Health Organisation), and the DSM-IV diagnostic criteria (the classification system published by the American Psychiatric Association). These relate particularly to very similar syndromes (groups of symptoms that together constitute a diagnosis) being given similar but different names or diagnostic labels. The labels 'ADHD' (DSM-IV) and 'Hyperkinetic Disorder' (ICD-10) illustrate this well.

There are also significant differences in the number of symptoms required to make a diagnosis and the way in which the behaviours and abnormalities are described.

Although at first glance these differences appear to be quite subtle and perhaps not very significant, clinical research and experience have shown that this is not the case.

The main differences between the two classification systems for ADHD/Hyperkinetic Disorder are:

1. DSM-IV classifies 'often talks excessively' as a symptom of hyperactivity. ICD-10 classifies a similar but more specific description of behaviour 'often talks excessively without response to social restraints' as a symptom of impulsivity

2. DSM-IV requires that six (or more) of the symptoms of 'hyperactivity–impulsivity' have persisted for at least six months to a degree that is maladaptive and inconsistent with expected developmental level. As it includes six symptoms of hyperactivity (and three of impulsivity) it is possible that children without any symptoms of lack of impulse control could fulfil the diagnostic criteria for ADHD. This is of particular interest at a time when current scientific opinion points towards the core deficit

of ADHD (and Hyperkinetic Disorder) being one of a deficit of impulse control.

The differences between the ICD-10 and DSM-IV diagnostic criteria result in each selecting a different but overlapping group of children. ICD-10 has been repeatedly shown to select a smaller group of children with more severe symptoms than those selected using DSM-IV.

In practice, it is important to note that there is indisputable evidence that the larger group of young people who meet the less stringent, more inclusive DSM-IV criteria have symptoms that are potentially disabling (and by definition, are causing significant impairment), and that these symptoms respond favourably to recognised treatment.

By insisting that ICD-10 diagnostic criteria are met before deciding to treat for ADHD, clinicians run the risk of depriving a proportion of children with significant impairment (who fulfil DSM-IV criteria but not those of ICD-10) of effective treatment and intervention.

Many clinicians base their decision to treat or not on a number of opinions, observations and check lists, and their own overall impression of the severity of the symptoms and the degree of impairment that the symptoms inflict on the child.

Evidence-based practice (using treatments and interventions that have been proven to be effective) is becoming mandatory. Utilisation of DSM-IV diagnostic criteria rather than ICD-10 carries an additional advantage: the majority of international research, particularly major, well-designed, multi-centre studies, is being carried out on patients who fulfil DSM-IV criteria. If UK clinicians wish to utilise the evidence yielded by these studies they will have to apply it to the same clinical population (i.e. that selected by DSM-IV diagnostic criteria).

CHAPTER 2

What are Children with ADHD Like?

The core symptoms of ADHD are hyperactivity, impulsiveness, and attention deficit. Studies have repeatedly shown that the symptoms of ADHD are remarkably stable over time. The core symptoms and patterns of behaviour will remain constant over weeks, months and years, although in about half of those children who are affected the symptoms will greatly diminish as they approach adult life.

CORE SYMPTOMS OF ADHD

- Inattention
- Hyperactivity
- Impulsivity

For the symptoms of ADHD to be of clinical significance and to fulfil the diagnostic criteria, they must be present in a significant number and to a sufficient degree to affect seriously a person's ability to function. They must also be present to an extent that exceeds what is normal for a person of that age and stage of development.

Talking with families and professionals working both in the UK and elsewhere in the world, it seems that there are common threads to the stories and experiences of many families living with ADHD, although every child and their family contains unique individuals with their own specific circumstances, advantages and dis-advantages. What follows is a description of the sorts of events, feelings, behaviours and reactions that could occur at different stages in the life of someone with ADHD and their family.

Children with ADHD are Hyperactive

It is normal for small children to appear hyperactive. Movement levels increase in all children until they are about three years old. After this age the level of normal movement reduces. There are reports of ADHD children being unusually active in the womb before they are born. They are sometimes rather difficult babies, who cry a lot and do not sleep well. Sometimes it is reported that the baby was difficult to warm to, perhaps did not enjoy physical contact.

Their parents may well have been seriously overtired and despondent; they may even be contending with their own ADHD symptoms. Babies who fit this description would not be the easiest or most pleasant children to rear, and it is highly likely that they would not experience their parents at their best. This early pattern of relationships could have far-reaching consequences. For many children with ADHD, their experience of early life is fortunately not as bad as this. They may have been noted to be overactive and have difficulty concentrating for as long as other children of their age, but it is often only when they enter school that their difficulties become obvious. For the first time in their lives they are required to sit still, engage in specific tasks and complete them. They start to stand out as different from other children.

ADHD children in school are frequently those who are not in their seats when they are supposed to be, or if they are, won't remain there for long. They are likely to be children who are constantly chattering, shouting out, intruding on others and preventing everyone else from doing what they are supposed to be doing. They tend to be disorganised, frequently forgetting essential equipment or losing it. Teachers often find this sort of behaviour irritating. Other children may initially accept it or find it amusing, but by the time the ADHD child has impulsively attacked them, or prevented them from learning, they will have started to find them irritating too.

Children with ADHD are Impulsive

It is currently thought that the core deficit in ADHD is in fact an inability to prevent response to impulse, both appropriate and inappropriate. This view has been championed by Professor Russell Barkley, an eminent American worker in the field of ADHD. He suggests that the core problem experienced by people with ADHD is that they experience profound and pervasive difficulties with impulsiveness, particularly in stopping themselves from responding to signals, stimuli, or events that are irrelevant to completing the task in hand.

Professor Michael Gordon describes this eloquently:

> Their problems of inattention are just one consequence of being unable to keep themselves from whatever may come down the proverbial 'pike', whether they be noises, ideas or loose threads on a sweater. The distractibility, inability to plan ahead, disorganisation, peer problems, the seeming inability to anticipate consequences at all, according to this notion, result from a primary problem of being unable to wait. At the heart of ADHD is the relative incapacity to keep from responding to whatever is most interesting or rewarding at the moment. (Gordon 1995, p.1.14)

This impulsivity, or acting without thinking about the possible consequences of their actions, causes children with ADHD and their families many difficulties. Parents have to be hyper-vigilant in order to prevent their child becoming involved in accidents. Road safety is a classic example of this. Many children with ADHD cannot be trusted to walk safely along the pavement unaccompanied, as other children of their age may be. Their parents know that if the child sees someone or something that catches their attention, they might cross a busy road without paying attention to on-coming traffic.

Other young people with ADHD may act on dares by their friends, partly spurred on by a desire for peer approval. Some young people have foolishly jumped from dangerous heights, or run into the road 'playing chicken' for this reason. Sometimes they will do things 'just to see what happens' or to satisfy their own curiosity.

Impulsivity can also contribute to difficulties in social situations, and make it very difficult to establish and maintain friendships. Butting in, saying the wrong thing without thinking, and thumping other children because they have the urge (but often not the justification to do so), may cause disasters on the social scene, resulting in a child who desperately wants friends being rejected.

Children with ADHD often have good or innocent intentions and yet appear to have indulged in deliberately antisocial or undesirable actions. Their actions are often confused with oppositional or anti-social acts, in which the child appears to be deliberately pursuing an undesirable course of action for negative reasons. It is true that after years of constant trouble and accusations, young people with ADHD do sometimes develop oppositional or anti-social patterns of behaviour. This could be interpreted in terms of their 'fulfilling a prophecy'.

Children with ADHD have Difficulty Paying Attention and Sustaining Concentration

Although children with ADHD are usually noteworthy because of the impulsivity and hyperactivity that makes them 'stand out' from their peers, the pervasive difficulties they experience because of a short attention span can have other far-reaching consequences. In particular, they find it extremely hard to learn. This applies not only to academic tasks, but to practical skills, motor skills (like learning to swim or to ride a bike), and, very important, in learning to speak (becoming involved in conversations and group activities).

Many of the 'disabilities' noted in children with ADHD, such as those related to scholastic and social skills, are due to an inability to concentrate for long enough to take on board and register what needs to be learnt. The children often have the innate ability to learn these skills, but until they are helped to sustain attention for long enough to do so, appear incapable of mastering them.

The cost of this inability to concentrate can be considerable, not only in terms of education and success at school, but also in terms of leading a normal happy existence with family and friends.

There is increasing concern for a number of children, particularly girls, who are not overtly hyperactive, impulsive or violent, but who quietly fail unnoticed, because of a very real and disabling deficit in their ability to concentrate. If this is noticed and treated such children can thrive. This is the group of children referred to as having ADD (ADHD without the hyperactivity).

Children with ADHD may have Problems Making Friends

Many children with ADHD find themselves with few friends, and often they are 'the wrong sort'. Children are painfully aware of this, and many would do anything to change, if only they knew how and were able to do so. Their difficulties often stem from impulsiveness and a short attention span that results in an inability to learn social rules easily, or to understand social cues.

Very often these children can be helped to succeed in social arenas if they are given extra help. They need to learn what the rest of us learnt successfully, often without thinking. Parents and teachers can often help with this in a tactful way. Specific and explicit instructions might be needed. For example: 'First you go and stand on the edge of a group of children. You stand quietly and listen for a while, very carefully. When you are sure that you know what they are talking about, and you have thought of something relevant to say, you wait for a suitable gap in the conversation and then say that you agree with what is being said because… or, that you have experience of that too…'

This might seem patronising, and thought must be given to delivering such help in a non-critical, supportive and positive way. It may, however, be an extremely positive way to help a lonely and willing child.

Repeated failures and rejection of a child by his or her peer group can have devastating consequences on the child's self-esteem and subsequent behaviour, so this is not an area to be neglected by parents or professionals, in either the assessment or the treatment of ADHD.

There are children whose behaviour has been so bad, as a consequence of their ADHD, that they have been effectively ostracised by others, because no one can tolerate their extremely disruptive and often violent behaviour. They may have been rejected by several child minders and nursery schools.

Children with ADHD may have Difficulties Learning

Hyperactivity, impulsiveness, and difficulties sustaining attention can seriously impair the child's ability to learn. They often, unless very bright, start to fall behind the rest of the class. In addition to being a behavioural nuisance, the child with ADHD develops academic problems – something else to worry about, and to be ridiculed and possibly punished for.

A significant proportion of children with ADHD also have specific learning difficulties. In particular, they tend to find reading and writing rather difficult. Because our educational system requires proficiency in reading and writing in order to participate effectively in all subjects, it is hardly surprising that these children frequently fail. Once they have fallen behind their peer group they find it extremely difficult to catch up. Not only do they find the medium in which knowledge is shared particularly difficult, they also have a mind that makes learning difficult. They can't concentrate for as long as their peer group. Noise and movement around them easily distracts them. They often miss critical information or instruction from the teacher, because they were thinking of something else at that time.

Many of them have the misfortune of having appallingly untidy handwriting. Unless their teacher appreciates the cause of their difficulties, their painstaking efforts that result in short, scruffy, untidy assignments, may receive criticism, or ridicule. This is especially so for children who also have dyspraxia (difficulty in the fine co-ordination of movement).

Research from the USA suggests that children with ADHD tend to exhibit the following learning problems:

° 90 per cent of children with ADHD are underproductive in schoolwork

° 90 per cent of children with ADHD underachieve at school

° 20 per cent of children with ADHD have reading difficulties

° 60 per cent of children with ADHD have serious handwriting difficulties

° 30 per cent of children with ADHD drop out of school in the USA

° 5 per cent of people with ADHD complete a four-year degree course in a college or university in the USA compared to approximately 25 per cent of the general population.

Children with ADHD may have Problems at Home

Children with ADHD may have difficulties at home. Their parents will often have tried literally every method they can think of to get their child to behave more appropriately. Relationships even within the most caring of families are likely to have been under enormous strain for many years. In the same way that ADHD rears its head at school, it will wreak havoc at home, affecting both people and property.

Children with ADHD often need less sleep than others do, with the result that everyone else becomes chronically tired, and parents get little time to themselves. Constant chatter, noise, movement, squabbles, and destruction of video recorders and 'all things valuable' are aspects of family life that many parents describe. Their children never seem to have a full set of anything; sometimes not even an intact toy.

Families often describe serious marital problems, at least partly as a consequence of their child's' ADHD symptoms. Sibling rivalry, a problem that affects many families anyway, can be augmented by the presence of ADHD. Sometimes there is more than one child within the family suffering from ADHD. Unaffected family members have a great deal to contend with. Parents become worn down by repeated calls from school as a result of their child's behaviour, and on occasions repeated exclusions from school. It can be very tempting to direct blame and recriminations towards the wrong people.

Parents often feel ostracised by their friends and families, as their child's behaviour has led them to be excluded from social events. They may feel that they are incompetent or lacking in skills; indeed some parents seen in ADHD clinics have been told so by relatives or professionals. Sometimes they are accused of trying to attribute their child's difficulties to medical causes to conceal their own inadequacies.

The consequences of ADHD and the situations outlined above are far reaching for all concerned, and should be taken into account when deciding how best to help.

Children with ADHD may have Other Problems

Neuropsychiatric Disorders

There is a strong overlap between the symptoms of ADHD and those of other neuropsychiatric and developmental disorders. These include:

- ° Autistic Spectrum Disorders (Autism and Asperger's Syndrome)

- ° Obsessive Compulsive Disorder

- ° Gilles de la Tourette's Syndrome

These disorders are described in the next chapter: 'Differential Diagnosis'.

Some of these conditions should be born in mind during assessment and treatment as they can mask other symptoms, making diagnosis difficult. Careful thought must be given when treating children who have ADHD and other conditions as treatment for one may adversely affect the other's symptoms. It is important that children with ADHD, especially when it is complicated by another condition, receive help from a doctor who has receive specialist training in child psychiatry, and who has knowledge about the interaction between drugs. Sometimes paediatricians will be able to look after such children if they have that expertise themselves, or if they work in conjunction with a child psychiatrist who can advise them.

Other Mental Health Difficulties

A lot of children with ADHD have other mental health problems which need to be recognised, distinguished from the core ADHD symptoms, and taken into account during assessment and treatment planning.

- ° 60 per cent of children with ADHD display *Oppositional Defiant Disorder:* losing their temper, arguing with adults, refusing to comply and deliberately annoying others

- ° 45 per cent of children with ADHD display *Conduct Disorder:* Chronic aggression towards others, destructive behaviour, deceitfulness or theft, serious and chronic rule breaking

- ° 25 per cent of children with ADHD display *antisocial or delinquent (i.e. criminal) behaviour*

- ° 33 per cent of children with ADHD experience *major clinical depression:* low mood, tearfulness, social withdrawal, altered sleep pattern, appetite loss?, behavioural problems, reduced attention and concentration span, loss of interests, on occasions suicidal thoughts

- ° 30 per cent of children with ADHD display clinically defined *anxiety disorders:* fear and avoidance of certain situations or encounters that take the form of fears or phobias, physical symptoms such as tummy ache, sickness, headaches, shortness of breath, fear of separation from parents, obsessional behaviour

- ° 50 per cent or more of children with ADHD display *emotional problems*

- ° 50 per cent or more of children with ADHD display *social skills problems.*

All these conditions can mask underlying ADHD, sometimes resulting in an incomplete or inaccurate diagnosis being made and inappropriate treatment being implemented.

As discussed in the chapter concerning the symptoms of ADHD, babies and children who have the core symptoms of ADHD have very significant problems in sustaining attention long enough to learn new skills, including the social skills necessary to form good relationships with others. In addition, the behaviour of young children with ADHD is often in itself difficult for parents to cope with. Some children with ADHD develop an Attachment Disorder, which makes it difficult for them to form secure relationships with others.

Some children with ADHD, particularly those who have Early-Onset Conduct Disorder (which involves serious problems such as fire-setting, thieving, assaulting with a weapon, lying, bullying), have a high risk of developing a drug or alcohol problem, or becoming involved in violent crime. Fortunately, despite these eventualities being parents' worst fears, most children with ADHD do not go this way. They appear, however, to start to smoke at an earlier age.

There is an increasing amount of information concerning the nature of the abuse of alcohol, nicotine and other illegal drugs by people who have ADHD. It seems that they are more likely to use these drugs, and to use them earlier in life than people without ADHD. They have an increased tendency to become both physically and psychologically dependent on them (addicted), and consequently are more likely to suffer from the harmful consequences of drug and alcohol misuse. However, research from the USA has shown that people with ADHD are more likely to use cannabis than stimulants or any of the other illegal drugs.

Symptoms of ADHD

Children with ADHD are hyperactive

Children with ADHD are impulsive

Children with ADHD have difficulty paying and sustaining attention

Associated Difficulties

Children with ADHD may have difficulty making friends

Children with ADHD may have difficulty learning

Children with ADHD may have problems at home

Other Disorders Associated with ADHD

The Autistic Spectrum Disorders (Autism and Asperger's Syndrome)

Obsessive Compulsive Disorder

Gilles de la Tourette's Syndrome

Oppositional Defiant Disorder

Conduct Disorder

Attachment Disorder

Depression

Anxiety

Substance abuse

CHAPTER 3

Other Conditions that May Look Like ADHD

Not every child who is hyperactive and impulsive, and has difficulty with attention and concentration, has ADHD. There are other medical and psychiatric conditions that can be mistaken for ADHD and the doctor needs to consider them whilst assessing a child who presents with these symptoms. Some of these conditions are described below.

Physical Disorders, Medications and Drugs that can Mimic ADHD Symptoms

   ° Impaired vision or hearing

   ° Seizures

   ° Sequelae of head trauma

   ° Acute or chronic medical illness

   ° Poor nutrition

   ° Insufficient sleep due to a sleep disorder or environment

   ° Side effects of medications and drugs.

Impaired Vision or Hearing

Difficulty in hearing (perhaps as a result of 'glue ear' following multiple ear infections) or seeing creates problems for children understanding what is being said to them and in making sense of what is going on around them. This leads to difficulty in making sense of what is happening and in learning. Consequently, children with these impairments can become confused, even despondent, and often have learning difficulties. Their unhappiness can become manifest in behavioural and emotional difficulties. Their actions often give the impression that the child can't or won't pay attention, or that they can't learn.

Freeman (1975) found that 20 per cent of deaf children had significant behaviour problems, with restlessness, dependency and aggression as prominent features. Other difficulties associated with deafness in childhood are cerebral palsy, visual impairment and cognitive delay.

Around 70 per cent of visually impaired children also have developmental delay, with additional difficulties such as learning difficulties and cerebral palsy being quite common. These can have radical impacts on children's ability to explore and investigate their surroundings, so their concepts of the external world are slow to develop. Visually impaired children tend to experience difficulty in developing a sense of themselves as distinct and separate individuals who relate to but are separate from other aspects of the environment. They may find concepts of time, separation and distance extremely hard to comprehend.

Freeman (1977), when reviewing available research findings, found that approximately 40 per cent of blind children showed moderate to severe signs of disturbance. Feeding and sleep disturbances are common in younger children. Social isolation and self-stimulatory behaviours, such as hand-flapping, rocking and eye-pressing were common in children, often as a result of sensory deprivation, anxiety or boredom. During adolescence, anxiety about social relationships and sexual interests are common.

Expert assessment and advice about appropriate interventions is required by parents of children with impaired vision and hearing, especially when it seems likely that the child also has additional difficulties, such as the symptoms of ADHD. The similarities between the symptoms if ADHD and the behaviours outlined above are self-evident. Of course some children with sensory impairments also have ADHD and this possibility should not be overlooked.

Seizures

Epilepsy, the most serious and common chronic neurological disorder in childhood, affects approximately 4 in 1000 children. Epileptic seizures in children can take many forms which are not comprehensively covered in this book. Although, in general, the symptoms of epilepsy do not bear a strong resemblance to those of epilepsy, the features or associated features of certain types of epilepsy and some of the medications commonly prescribed to treat it (anticonvulsant or anti-epileptic medication) do echo some of the core features of ADHD. These include reduced attention span, disturbed behaviour and restlessness.

Many studies have shown that children with epilepsy have an increased risk of psychiatric disturbance, compared to other children with no other physical or neurological disorder, e.g. the Isle of Wight Study (Rutter *et al.* 1970). Early research suggested that children with epilepsy could be regarded as examples of 'brain-damaged' children, with a characteristic pattern of disturbance including overactivity, impulsivity, aggression and distractibility – the core symptoms of ADHD. These children were thought to have 'epileptic personalities'. More recent work by Rutter *et al.* (1970), Stores (1978) and Hoare (1984) has shown that the most disturbed children with epilepsy have the same range and type of psychopathology as other children. The concept of the epileptic child has therefore been abandoned. Hoare and Kerley (1991) have recently established that the commonest forms of disturbance are emotional or neurotic disorders, a finding not previously recognised.

Seizures can lead to disorders through a variety of mechanisms, and some of these disorders can give the initial impression of having some of the features of ADHD:

1. Neurological factors, relating to the brain abnormality that gives rise to the seizures, and the seizures themselves can cause a number of difficulties.

    Frequent undiagnosed absence seizures (grand mal) can give the impression that the child is having momentary lapses of attention staring into space. The child can't stop these attacks and could be accused of not trying to concentrate and pay attention. Because they are completely unaware of what has been going on around them during the attack they have also missed out completely on what was happening at the time, which can make learning extremely difficult. This type of seizure can occur frequently – some children may experience as many as 80–100 per day. Such seizures, once correctly identified, usually respond well to appropriate medication.

    Grand mal, (also called tonic–clonic seizures), in addition to causing the obvious loss of consciousness and symptoms and complications, often cause the affected child to be drowsy, and 'off colour' for some time after the seizure has finished. This experience can last up to several days. During this time the child can find it extremely difficult to sustain attention and to learn and may display altered behaviour patterns. Other children experience similar symptoms and difficulties over days and hours preceding seizures.

    Some children experience abnormal electrical brain activity, not sufficient to give rise to the signs and symptoms that usually characterise epileptic seizures, but sufficient to cause disturbed thinking, learning and behaviour.

    Epileptic seizures that arise in the temporal lobes of the brain can give rise to seizures in which consciousness is variably affected, but the subject displays unusual behaviour or experiences abnormal perceptions.

Sometime it can be quite difficult to identify epilepsy as the true cause of such disturbances.

2. Individual characteristics of the child, for example impulsivity or distractibility, or cognitive (thinking) or learning difficulties, act as risk factors for psychiatric disorders in children with epilepsy.

3. Stressful effects of chronic illness, such as parents feeling reluctant to allow their child to become more independent, or parental/marital disharmony resulting from differing views on how best to handle the child, can inadvertently give rise to complex behavioural responses in the child. If they are subjected to prejudice or stigma as a result of having epilepsy children can often become unhappy, depressed or behaviourally disturbed, displaying a wide range of potential symptoms that need careful evaluation.

4. Anticonvulsant medication, particularly older drugs such as Phenobarbitone, can have significant side effects, often producing symptoms of overactivity, irritability and depression. Others, such as Carbamazepine or Sodium Valproate can adversely affect alertness, concentration and attention.

    It is important to bring this to the attention of the doctor treating the child's epilepsy, as anticonvulsant medication should not be abruptly withdrawn. Withdrawal should always be under medical supervision as it can lead to potentially serious complications since lack of control over epilepsy may emerge.

Some children have both epilepsy and ADHD. There are important interactions between medications to consider, and the stimulant drugs (e.g. Ritalin, often used in the treatment of ADHD) can lower the brain's seizure threshold, making the child more vulnerable to increased epileptic seizure attacks. However, there is increasing evidence to suggest that stimulant medications are not necessarily inappropriate for some children with epilepsy and ADHD. This is particularly the case for those who have been fortunate, and have found that medication has completely controlled and halted their epileptic seizures. Prescribing for such children needs careful thought and a very experienced doctor.

Sequelae of Head Injury

The victims of head injury in childhood do not represent a random cross section of children: some children are more likely than others to sustain such an injury. Boys, especially those who are hyperkinetic (overactive, hyperactive), those with learning difficulties and those with below average intelligence are particularly vulnerable, as are those who, for whatever reason, are poorly supervised.

The type of head injury and the location and severity of consequent brain damage will influence the type of symptoms that the child will experience.

Open head injuries, in which the skull is penetrated, e.g. by gun shot, tend to result in localised brain damage and can cause epilepsy. Whichever part of the brain is injured, it seems that the effect on performance IQ (the ability to complete tasks and to solve problems) is greater than on verbal IQ (the ability to express oneself in, and comprehend, language).

Closed injuries, which are more common, are frequently the result of acceleration/deceleration and rotation, often during a road traffic accident or a fall. These typically involve widespread brain damage and are more likely to result in prolonged unconsciousness and post-traumatic amnesia or PTA (loss of memory of events for a period immediately following the injury).

While there remains some doubt as to whether or not mild head injuries are innocuous, there is no doubt that severe head injuries result in cognitive impairment (difficulties with thought processes) and psychiatric problems (Rutter *et al.* 1983, Middleton 1989).

Closed head injuries that result in at least two weeks of PTA commonly result in cognitive impairment (again affecting performance IQ more than verbal IQ). Recovery may be partial, and is often slow, with improvements occurring fastest during the year following the accident, although progress at a slower pace can occur over a much longer time scale.

The short-term consequence of head injuries often occur in three overlapping phases: an early phase of confusion, regression or denial; a middle phase of demanding and arrogant behaviour, or listlessness and depression; and a final phase of gradual accommodation to injury (Hill 1989).

The longer-term psychiatric disorders seen in about half the victims of open and closed head injuries usually involve emotional and conduct problems. Children who had minor emotional or behavioural difficulties prior to the accident are particularly vulnerable to such disorders. Other pre-existing adversities faced by their families (e.g. overcrowding) can compound this. Parents often, quite understandably, become increasingly overprotective and reluctant to discipline their child. This too can exacerbate any other difficulties.

Severe closed head injuries can result in a distinct syndrome of social disinhibition: a child may, for example, become unduly outspoken, ask embarrassing questions, make very personal comments or get undressed in inappropriate situations. Children may also become forgetful, overtalkative, impulsive and careless about their own cleanliness and appearance.

The symptoms of ADHD can be seen to occur as a result of head injuries – indeed, they might have been the cause of the accident. Careful assessment of the child's difficulties by clinician(s) familiar with such injuries will facilitate the offer of comprehensive and effective help for the child and his or her family.

Acute or Chronic Medical Illness

Children with chronic illnesses are twice as likely to be disturbed as healthy children with psychological disturbance rates varying from 33 per cent of children with central nervous system disease, to 12 per cent of children with asthma or diabetes. The sorts of disturbances seen are the same as those experienced by 'normal, healthy' children. This suggests that the mechanism by which chronically ill children develop such difficulties is not specific to the illness, and could be interpreted to be result of the stress and difficulty imposed on the family by the illness (Rutter 1970).

It is conceivable that some of the symptoms of ADHD could arise during or following an illness. One important differentiating factor between symptoms as a result of illness and true symptoms of ADHD, is that ADHD is a disorder that affects children throughout their development: one would expect them to have experienced ADHD symptoms before their illness.

Following a diagnosis of a severe illness, it is normal for the child and family to experience grief, as a reaction. This can also be the case when a diagnosis of a mental health or developmental disorder, such as ADHD or depression, is made. Typically, this will involve a number of phases of responses, through which most people pass, albeit at different rates. It is possible for a person to become stuck in one of these phases, apparently incapable of moving on. The first phase is usually a period of shock and disbelief, an intense emotional arousal immediately following the disclosure of the diagnosis.

This is usually rapidly followed by a period of denial, inability or unwillingness to accept the seriousness or likely outcome of the illness. This response is initially adaptive, as it allows the parent and child to gradually recognise the implications of what is happening. If this phase persists difficulties can arise, as families become unable to make the adjustments and changes necessary to cope with the consequences of the illness and its treatment.

In turn, this is followed by a period of sadness or anger. The child and family, as they register the implications and effects of the illness, start to look for explanations and can become very angry and bitter towards anyone or anything that they believe has been responsible for what has happened. Sad responses usually elicit sympathy from medical staff, whereas anger, particularly when it is directed towards the staff who are now having to treat the illness, can be very difficult for everyone to deal with.

Usually, if the grief reaction is successfully worked through, the child and family eventually accept what has happened and make the necessary adjustments in order to cope with whatever difficulties are encountered.

The ability to adjust to illness and disability is affected by a number of factors, including:

- ° *Predisposing factors:* e.g. the temperament of the child and their family members, the way that stress is experienced and dealt with, the family response and ability to cope, and societal and cultural responses

- ° *Precipitating factors:* e.g. whether the illness or disability had a rapid or insidious onset, and the severity of the stressful response

- ° *Perpetuating factors:* including the family and societies response to the illness or disability, potential reinforcement of illness role, and the possibility of an enduring stressful response to what has happened

- ° *Protective factors:* such as adaptive temperamental characteristics, harmonious relationships and peer-group support (Hoare 1993).

Illness can have many effects on a child's thoughts, behaviour and emotions. An unpredictable illness, such as poorly controlled epileptic seizures can make certain activities hazardous (e.g. swimming, riding a bike) and limit a child's ability to participate in a 'normal' life. The impairment that accompanies cerebral palsy can make control of movement (e.g. when writing, or playing sport) exceptionally difficult. Asthma can limit the type and amount of exercise a child can take. Persistent enuresis (bed wetting) can make it impossible to visit friends and participate in sleepovers. The persistent impulsive actions of children with severe ADHD can make it impossible for their parents to allow them to go out alone or unsupervised, at an age when their peers are allowed a much greater degree of independence.

Parents often respond to their child's illness or disability by becoming overcautious or overprotective, sometimes inhibiting the child's ability to join in with other children and limiting their capacity to enjoy as normal a life as possible. The need for hospital visits, attendance at clinics and medication can also place limitations on the child and family, and lead to difficulties in making appropriate adjustments.

Poor Nutrition

The period of maximum brain growth occurs between early foetal life and 12 months of age. It is therefore likely that the effects of malnutrition will be greatest when experienced in the first year of life. The deleterious effects of malnutrition on later intellectual development in the Third World are well recognised.

In developed western societies, early malnutrition is usually not due to lack of food, but to faulty feeding practices and factors within the child, such as faulty oral-motor dysfunction (poor co-ordination of the muscles used during feeding). Children, who fail to grow as expected during the first year of life, have an increased rate of developmental delay and of learning difficulties as well as a higher rate of emotional and behavioural difficulties (Skuse 1989).

The consequences of missing breakfast and having insufficient food on children's ability to learn have received a fair amount of interest, and most adults are familiar with the difficulties encountered in maintaining concentration and keeping an even temper when really hungry. For this reason it is important to ensure that children receive appropriate and adequate food at regular times.

Insufficient Sleep Due to Sleep Disorder or Environment

Chronic sleep deprivation can make it very difficult for a child to concentrate, learn and appear motivated. The child may also become irritable, bad tempered and miserable.

There are some well-recognised sleep disorders that can adversely affect children's sleep, including night-terrors and nightmares. Noisy bedrooms, the intrusion of others, too much light (e.g. from street lamps through thin curtains), shared or uncomfortable beds, and cold or excessive heat can all interrupt a child's sleep.

If sleep deprivation is felt to be a possible explanation for a child's behaviour careful exploration of the possibilities outlined above, and assessment and treatment of any underlying disorders, should be carried out.

Side Effects of Medications and Drugs

A number of prescribed and illegal medications and drugs can cause side effects that mimic the symptoms of ADHD. Some drugs, such as the anticonvulsant medications used to treat epileptic seizures (see above), commonly cause side effects that appear to be symptoms of ADHD, such as reduced attention and concentration, irritability, and difficulties thinking.

Other medications can also produce side effects that look like some of the symptoms of ADHD. For example, some anti-depressants, such as Amitriptyline, are sedative and can result in drowsiness. This, at first glance can give a false impression of reduced concentration span and distractibility. Salbutamol, used to treat asthma, can induce nervous agitation in the form of anxiety-like symptoms when given in larger doses.

In practice, it is hard to predict which side effects may affect a child when prescribing different medications. There are well-recognised side effect profiles for all prescribed drugs, and these are listed in the *British National Formulary, MIMS Magazine* and the *ABTA Data Sheet Compendium,* in addition to certain Internet web sites. These are widely available, and doctors and pharmacists will have the most recent editions. It is not uncommon for a child to appear to have a symptom which is not usually recognised as a side effect of the medication, although all available evidence suggests that it is the case. Your doctor will complete a form and send it to the CSM (Committee for the Safety of Medicines) if he or she believes that your child is experiencing an undocumented side effect.

It is really important that parents do not decide to stop any prescribed medication abruptly, without first consulting a pharmacist and their GP. This is especially true for medications used to treat serious conditions such as asthma and epilepsy. However, there are many effective alternative ways of treating these disorders.

It should also be remembered that some of the medications used to treat ADHD can actually exacerbate the symptoms they were intended to treat. This may occur if they are given in doses that are inappropriate for the child, or at sub-optimal dose intervals. For example, the child may suffer rebound hyperactivity when blood levels of stimulant medication fall too rapidly. These effects are discussed further in Chapter 9 on medications for ADHD.

Some illegal drugs, such as cannabis, can lead to a reduced attention span and difficulties thinking. Alcohol can also produce some symptoms reminiscent of ADHD.

In trying to decide whether the child or young person's symptoms are the result of medication or illicit drugs, or whether in fact they represent ADHD, a crucial consideration is timing. If the symptoms are related in time to when the drug was started or to the timing of the dose, it is likely that they are a response to that drug. If the symptoms predate the use of that medication or drug it is more likely that ADHD could lie behind the symptoms.

Psychiatric Disorders that could be Mistaken for ADHD

There are a number of conditions that have certain symptoms or behaviours that characterise them or are frequently associated with them, which can lead parents and professionals wrongly to believe that a child has ADHD. These are outlined below.

It is very important to note that in real life, child psychiatrists recognise that not every child fits neatly into a diagnostic category. Some children have features of two or more disorders, for example ADHD and Gilles de la Tourette's Syndrome. Recent research and psychiatric thinking suggest that these disorders and other neuropsychiatric conditions (such as Obsessive Compulsive Disorder and the Autistic Spectrum Disorders) might be related, because certain symptom constellations recur together in many children (Gillberg *et al.* 1983).

It is important to look hard for symptoms of other conditions that appear to be either related to, or associated with ADHD, as the presence of each will affect the manifestation of the other, and there are serious implications relating to management that need to be taken into account. This is particularly relevant when the symptoms of one disorder are very prominent. For example, it would perhaps be understandable if mild–moderate symptoms of ADHD were missed in an initial assessment if a child presented with prominent and distressing motor and vocal tics – a consequence of Gilles de la Tourettes' Syndrome. The ADHD symptoms might be causing the child significant difficulties and impairment and would be worthy of treatment, even though the prominent and very obvious signs the Gilles de la Tourettes' Syndrome were the reason for the child attending for an assessment in the first place.

Autistic Spectrum Disorders (Autism and Asperger's Syndrome)

Disorders across this spectrum involve difficulties of varying degrees with social skills, sharing emotions, relationships and communication. People with these disorders tend to have a need to the preserve sameness and adhere to rituals. They may have very narrow fixed interests or 'obsessions', and may have isolated talents present to an extraordinary degree. Three-quarters of autistic individuals have an IQ below 70, with a significant proportion of them never acquiring useful speech. There is also a strong association with epilepsy. These disabilities and symptoms are present from early childhood, and persist. However, in some children these symptoms develop after a period of apparently normal development.

These difficulties give rise to unusual and complex patterns of behaviour. Each child is different, and as in ADHD an individual's symptom profile will evolve over time. Very often parents and professionals notice a child that seems to be in a world of their own. They do not play or interact in the same way as other children, and when anxious or distressed often become extremely hyperactive and possibly aggressive. They experience difficulties in understanding and using language, and interpreting what is going on in their environment. Their behaviour may show an initial similarity to that of a child with ADHD, although on closer inspection it usually becomes clear that the core difficulties and deficits are quite different. To complicate matters further, a significant proportion of children with Autistic Spectrum disorders also have symptoms of ADHD, which may need to be treated. Some of these children respond favourably to Ritalin or other stimulants, while others experience adverse side effects or fail to respond. This latter group will need further consideration by doctors experienced in treating children with Autistic Spectrum Disorders.

Obsessive Compulsive Disorder

The sufferer becomes disabled by a need to perform certain acts, rituals or to think particular thoughts. These needs are recognised by the sufferer to be unreasonable or even foolish, but their attempts to prevent themselves from carrying out the actions or rituals result in increasing and unbearable tension. These symptoms are often associated with depression. Again, the consequences of this disorder, particularly their preoccupation with their rituals/thoughts, can give the impression that the sufferer has difficulty with attention span. The need to comply with the thoughts and rituals can also create the impression of difficulty with both getting organised and planning activities, and with the control of impulses.

Gilles de la Tourette's Syndrome

This syndrome involves marked difficulties with repetitive involuntary jerking movements of the body (particularly the head and neck, although any muscle group could be affected), which the patient finds extremely difficult to prevent. Attempts to do so result in increasing tension. These are called motor tics. In Gilles de la Tourette's Syndrome they occur with sudden outbursts of noises – coughs or foul language – called vocal tics. These symptoms usually emerge at around the age of eight, and in some people persist into adult life.

Such symptoms often have a marked impact on the sufferer's ability to sustain attention, and can give a mistaken impression of hyperactivity. Children with tics often try to mask the repetitive nature of their tics by disguising them in part of a more complex, fidgeting or writhing pattern of behaviour. Gilles de la Tourette's syndrome can also occur with ADHD, so the involvement of a child and adolescent psychiatrist in the assessment and diagnosis of such complicated cases is essential. Motor tics can occur without the vocal tics, and still cause considerable difficulties.

Conduct Disorder

This disorder is characterised by a repetitive and persistent pattern of antisocial, aggressive or defiant conduct. Such behaviour is more severe than ordinary childish mischief or adolescent rebelliousness. Many young people with Conduct Disorder also have associated Specific Learning Disabilities, particularly with reading and writing. The consequences of these additional problems, occurring with oppositional, aggressive and antisocial behaviour, can lead to a pattern of symptoms that resembles ADHD, which diagnosis could then be missed.

It is important to bear in mind that there is a sub-group of children with ADHD who also have Conduct Disorder that begins in middle childhood. Conduct Disorder that starts well before teenage years is recognised to be almost exclusively associated with ADHD, and to have a high incidence of poor long-term outcome. This is in sharp contrast to Conduct Disorder that starts later in adolescence, and which is usually time-limited and has a better outcome. Children with Early-Onset Conduct Disorder and ADHD are also likely to have Specific Learning Difficulties (especially with reading and writing), which will make learning and maintaining their status within their peer group extremely difficult.

Because of the difficulties involved in accurately distinguishing Conduct Disorder from ADHD, and the fact that the two disorders frequently co-exist, a very careful psychiatric assessment is essential, and the assistance of the school together with the expertise of an educational psychologist is invaluable. This applies particularly to children presenting with Early-Onset Conduct Disorder, as research and clinical experience has clearly demonstrated that they are highly likely to have ADHD as well. When these children remain untreated there is a real risk of their going on to develop a pattern of repeated and violent behaviour.

Attachment Disorder

Children who have had difficult, repeated or prolonged separations from their parents or who have had very troubled relationships with them may present with Attachment Disorders. These children often appear to have many of the symptoms of ADHD, in that they show symptoms of poor self-control and a short attention span, and can be overly trusting and sociable. Distinguishing between Attachment Disorders and ADHD can be extremely difficult, and the two disorders often co-exist, magnifying the difficulties they each cause.

Depression and Other Emotional Problems

These include persistent low mood, unhappiness, a negative outlook on life, disturbed sleep and appetite, difficulty in thinking and concentrating, irritability, social withdrawal, anxiety, and, on occasion, suicidal thoughts. People who are depressed frequently have significant and disabling difficulties with sustaining attention, and in working to their usual standards. This normally resolves completely when they recover from depression. It is particularly important to consider whether the symptoms of depression came on before or after difficulties with attention were noticed.

It is important that these disorders are not missed during the assessment of the child. Prescribing medication, particularly stimulants, for children who have Depression or emotional problems but who do not have ADHD could be harmful.

If the assessing doctor is not sure whether the child's symptoms could be caused by an Attachment or other emotional disorder they should discuss the case fully with an experienced child psychiatrist and/or psychotherapist. It is sometimes difficult to decide if the child has ADHD, depression, an Attachment Disorder, or a combination of these three. The doctor needs to be quite certain that the diagnosis is right if they are to relieve the child's symptoms effectively. The presence of any one of these disorders has a significant impact on the treatment of the others.

Anxiety Disorders

The child experiences severe anxiety, for example when separated from their parents or in relation to school or social situations. The effects of anxiety could easily be attributed to a persistent deficit in attention. An anxious child could be preoccupied with, and distracted by, other worries; which results in real difficulties in sustaining attention on other matters. Their worries and agitation often make it difficult for them to remain on task, and they may fidget and appear to be hyperactive.

Psychotic Disorders

Although these are very rare conditions in children and adolescents it is necessary to keep them in mind when assessing young people that are unable to concentrate. People suffering with a psychotic disorder lose touch with reality. They may not be able to distinguish between what is going on in their head (which has the appearance of being real to them), and external reality, as experienced by everyone else. They often complain of voices, hallucinations, and disturbing thoughts, which they perceive and believe to be true and real. Such thoughts and beliefs are called delusions. The young person is usually not able to concentrate, and although they can give the impression of having an attention problem they are more seriously ill and need urgent assessment and treatment by a psychiatrist.

Conditions that May Mimic ADHD
Physical Conditions
° Impaired vision or hearing
° Seizures
° Sequelae of head trauma
° Acute or chronic medical illness
° Poor nutrition
° Insufficient sleep
Medication and Illicit Drugs
° Phenobarbitol
° Carbamazepine
° Alcohol
° Illegal drugs
Psychiatric Disorders
° Conduct Disorder
° Depression and other emotional disorders
° Anxiety disorders
° Obsessive Compulsive Disorder
° Gilles de la Tourette's Syndrome
° Autism, Asperger's Syndrome
° Psychotic Disorder
° Behavioural disorders such as Opposition Defiant and Conduct disorders

CHAPTER 4

How Common is ADHD?

Although figures vary according to where in the world the studies were carried out, the populations studied, and the diagnostic criteria used, it seems that ADHD is present throughout the world in about 1–5 per cent of the population. Figures for the UK, according to Professor Taylor (The Institute of Psychiatry and the Maudsley Hospital, London) suggest that about 1.7 per cent of the British population has ADHD in its more severe form.

It is well known that studies carried out by clinicians utilising DSM-IV diagnostic criteria have revealed higher rates of ADHD (3–5%) than have studies which used ICD-10 (approximately 0.5%). Whilst it has been argued that DSM-IV criteria are over-inclusive, there is also evidence that children who satisfy those criteria also benefit significantly from treatment, and should therefore receive appropriate interventions.

It appears that boys outnumber girls, although it is also believed that boys are more likely to be identified because they are more likely to be violent, and consequently to be noticed to have difficulties. According to Professor Taylor's research, boys attend ADHD clinics more frequently than girls, with a ratio of 2.5:1. If children with learning disability are taken into consideration this ratio falls to 1.9:1. It is interesting to see that Australian studies show a much higher ratio of boys to girls than British studies (10:1).

There have been a number of studies that have attempted to compare the rates of ADHD in different countries and in urban and rural communities. Studies by both Shen, and Luk and Leung, show that nearly three times more Chinese boys than English boys score positively for ADHD.

It is thought that only approximately one in ten children with ADHD in Britain has been identified and is currently receiving help. The undiagnosed children and their families are presumably experiencing unnecessary difficulties and problems that are potentially treatable.

CHAPTER 5

Evolutionary and Biological Explanations of ADHD

ADHD is not 'a hysterical condition originating in America'. There is a wealth of scientific knowledge that gives us some understanding of the causes of the symptoms of ADHD.

The term Attention Deficit Hyperactivity Disorder refers to a syndrome in which sufferers present with a characteristic set of symptoms. There are several potential mechanisms that could result in these symptoms. The effects of *nature* (such as the child's brain chemistry, function or genetic make-up) and *nurture* (such as their life experiences, social environment and the way in which they have been parented), are intricately interrelated and have far-reaching consequences. The causes of any child or adult's symptoms are usually multi-factorial. ADHD is a classic example of a bio-psycho-social disorder. The symptoms are a result of an individual's unique biology, psychological make-up, life experiences and environment.

There are a number of interesting theories that attempt to explain ADHD along anthropological lines, which help us to understand why so many people have symptoms of attention deficit, hyperactivity and poor impulse control, and why they find certain environments and occupations more difficult than others.

The Hunters and Farmers Theory

Thom Hartmann suggests that 200,000 years ago, before the agricultural revolution, the symptoms of ADHD, now considered to be a disadvantage in modern society, would have conferred a significant advantage on those who had them. A nomadic hunter would need constantly to scan his environment for signs of prey. He would have to be able to drop whatever he had been doing before being distracted by the prey and chase it immediately. If he and his family were to eat that day, he would not have had time to think of any risks he may have been taking. Aggression and impulsiveness could similarly have conferred a distinct advantage.

Following the agricultural revolution, a completely different set of behavioural characteristics became more advantageous. Men now needed to plan their actions far more carefully. No longer could they rush off in pursuit of prey whenever it caught their eye. As farmers they needed carefully and perhaps laboriously to prepare their land and sow, tend, and reap their crops at a pace and time scale dictated by the seasons and weather.

The theory proposed by Thom Hartmann has been taken up and developed by others, and currently forms the centre of a fascinating on-going academic debate, which focuses on the apparent links between information from anthropology, neuroscience, psychology and the social sciences. This debate is enabling us at last to start to make sense of the complex causation of ADHD.

Evolution, Biology, and ADHD as a Disorder of Adaptation

A pivotal paper was published by Peter Jenson of the National Institute of Mental Health in Rockville, USA, and several eminent colleagues, in the *Journal of the American Academy of Child and Adolescent Psychiatry,* in December 1997.

The authors examine the concept of ADHD in relation to evolutionary theories of biology and psychology. They examine the contribution of the core symptoms of attention deficit, impulsivity and hyperactivity to adaptation, depending on the environment the child finds himself in. They argue that ADHD occurs at too high a frequency (approximately 3–5%) in the general population to represent a disease that would by definition place those who have it at a disadvantage. They suggest that the symptoms of ADHD must place those who possess them at some sort of evolutionary advantage, albeit under a specific set of circumstances.

The child with ADHD is described as a 'response-ready' individual. This means that their behaviour is characterised as being:

° Hypervigilant (or very alert), with the ability to retrieve and integrate information through all their senses at once.

° Rapid-scanning.

° Quick to pounce (or flee).

° Hyperactive (foraging for food, moving towards warmer climes as seasons and ice-ages come and go).

The 'response-ready' individual would be at an advantage under brutal or harsh physical conditions, for example in frozen steppe or humid jungles. In contrast, people with less marked traits of this nature, being essentially contemplative, would be 'environmentally challenged'.

Within a 'hunter-gatherer' society, people with 'response-ready' characteristics would have been successful warriors, whilst those with more contemplative characteristics would have made use of their abilities in long-term planning, strategic operations, or the development of novel solutions to environmental challenges.

Jenson and his colleagues argue that because society has become more industrialised and organised, and generally safer, with food more plentiful, the 'response ready' traits of ADHD now confer less of an advantage. In modern societies successful people are more likely to be those who are able to show ability in:

° Problem solving and analytical skills.

° The restraint of impulsivity.

° The control of hyperactivity.

A significant number of people in our society, who display characteristics of ADHD, find themselves labelled as having a disorder.

Viewed from an evolutionary perspective, our current school environment (or many work situations) could hardly be more difficult for the 'response-ready' child. We know that by altering the school environment over a period (e.g. by altering seating arrangements, having smaller classes, and more 'hands-on' learning) it is possible to alter significantly the behaviour patterns and responses of the 'response-ready' child. They are then able to learn and function more effectively in our modern society.

By reframing a disordered child with ADHD as 'experience-seeking, alert and curious', and adapting their environment to suit their abilities better, parents and professionals can teach them to cope more easily. They can be helped to extend their range of skills, enabling them to increase their ability to stay on task, inhibit their impulse and urges to move about, and improve their self-awareness. This is crucial if the child is to succeed rather than suffer gradual erosion of self-esteem, motivation, and disability.

It might be possible that by altering a 'response-ready' child's early environment, we could bring about long-standing changes in their ability to sustain attention, control their impulses and reduce unnecessary movement. This is the premise upon which many psychological and educational interventions for ADHD are based. An important question remains to be answered: 'At what point in the child's development are such interventions most likely to be effective?'

Neurones (brain cells) have the ability to alter and adapt their connections with other brain cells according to use and lack of use. This process is called 'plasticity', and involves laying down neuronal circuits that will govern the way a child's brain and behaviour will function in the future. It is likely that there are periods during a child's development when their neurones have greater plasticity.

The formation of neuronal circuits in the child's brain continues into their twenties. It involves both genetically pre-determined growth of brain structures and a degree of 'fine-tuning' of the connections between brain structures as result of use and disuse. This in turn occurs as a result of the experiences the child encounters in their environment.

Jenson and his colleagues have examined the way in which evolutionary, biological, psychological and social factors could account for the signs and symptoms we see in children with ADHD. They have tentatively proposed a theory of how these factors might interact both in the causation and solution of difficulties.

The debate that has ensued from their work has provoked a great deal of thought. It becomes possible to conceive the potential far-reaching consequences of the evolutionary and biological mechanisms at play. It is possible that these mechanisms explain not only the core symptoms of ADHD and their possible resolution, but also the more complex and intricate issues around the establishment of attachments to, and relationships with other people, amongst other aspects of social learning.

If people with ADHD choose their career and lifestyle appropriately, the traits of ADHD can still be a distinct advantage. It has been noted that certain careers are particularly suitable and rewarding for people with ADHD, who are said to be over-represented amongst Accident and Emergency Doctors, Combat Soldiers, Entrepreneurs, Aircraft Pilots, the New York Police Force...

These are jobs that require the ability to think and act very quickly according to rapidly changing circumstances, often in the absence of a set routine. A career that involved a lot of repetitive, rather tedious activities would be a disaster zone for someone with ADHD!

CHAPTER 6

Scientific Evidence about the Causes of ADHD

When considering the causes of the symptoms of ADHD from a purely scientific point of view it is necessary to draw on knowledge and ongoing research from a number of disciplines, including:

- ° anthropology
- ° genetics
- ° neuroanatomy
- ° neurophysiology
- ° neurochemistry
- ° dietetics and toxicology
- ° psychology
- ° the social sciences.

The contributions that these scientific disciplines are able to make enable us to start to understand the complex mechanisms behind ADHD, and facilitate the development of effective interventions that can be utilised to enable children and people with ADHD to succeed.

Genetics

There is a great deal of evidence to suggest that ADHD is an inherited disorder. A study by Dr Biederman and his colleagues at

Massachusetts General Hospital in 1990 looked at 457 first-degree relatives (biological parents or siblings) of 75 children with ADHD. They compared them with the families of 26 children with other psychiatric disorders and 26 control children (those with no mental health problem). They established that 25 per cent of the first-degree relatives of children with ADHD also had the disorder. This compared with only 5 per cent of first-degree relatives of the control group of children with other mental health disorders. This represents a 500 per cent increase in risk to other members of the family with an ADHD child.

Twin studies, in which researchers compare the rates of a disorder in both members of pairs of identical twins (who will possess identical genes and often very similar life circumstances) have shown that as many as 80–90 per cent of twin pairs in which one child has ADHD, both have ADHD. Studies of non-identical twin pairs (fraternal twins, with very similar life circumstances but only 25 per cent of genetic material in common) have shown that 32 per cent of twin pairs both have ADHD which is 6–10 times greater than that seen among unrelated children, where the prevalence of ADHD is 3–5 per cent.

These results add weight to the belief that the symptoms of ADHD are often genetically inherited, and that in many cases the child's environment and up-bringing do not in their own right account for the symptoms.

More recent studies have revealed that when considering the risk of inheriting ADHD from a second-degree relative, there is a greater chance of inheriting the condition from male relatives such as grandfathers and uncles, than from female relatives such as grandmothers and aunts.

There is increasing evidence that several genes are involved in the genetic transmission of ADHD. Studies carried out by Comings in California suggest that a spectrum of inter-related and overlapping disorders (such as ADHD, Gilles de la Tourette's Syndrome, Conduct Disorder, and Oppositional Defiant Disorder) are likely to be the result of shared genetic anomalies (Comings 1990).

Further work has suggested that a particular form of the gene for the Dopamine D4 Receptor might account for the altered patterns of brain activity seen in ADHD. It seems that there are many variations of this gene in the community, and that people with ADHD have a high incidence of one particular variant of the gene.

It is possible that increasing knowledge of the genetic mechanisms involved in the causation of the symptoms of ADHD might lead to advances in future treatments and the possible development of diagnostic tests.

Neuroanatomy: Is ADHD the Result of Structural Abnormality in the Brain?

Volumetric Nuclear Magnetic Resonance (known as MRI) scans have allowed researchers, with the help of computers, to calculate the volume of various structures in the brain. The caudate nucleus is a mass of nerve bundles situated in the brain which is concerned with the initiation and performance of voluntary movement. Results found by Hynd and his colleagues at the University of Georgia imply that the right-sided caudate nucleus in people with ADHD is larger than their left-sided one, and smaller than the caudate nuclei of normal children.

The caudate nucleus is one of the brain structures that control voluntary movement, and is made up of several bundles of nerve fibres, one of which is called the striatum. The striatum is important in inhibiting behaviour and sustaining attention. It has important neurological links with the limbic system (another brain structure/system), which is responsible for a variety of functions, including controlling emotions, motivation and memory.

The structural abnormalities within the brain described above are more common in boys. These findings point towards the possibility of the left-sided caudate nucleus in children with ADHD being involved in the causations and symptoms of ADHD, perhaps being less well developed.

More recent studies published by this team have shown that children with ADHD have slightly smaller areas of brain matter in the right frontal region. The frontal region of the brain has numerous functions, some of which involve task planning and impulse control. There are important connections from the frontal regions to the limbic system, which as described above, represents the emotional centre of the brain.

Hynd and his colleagues also showed that the corpus callosum was somewhat smaller in children with ADHD than in those who did not have ADHD. The corpus callosum is a band of nerve cells that connects one side of the brain to the other, allowing the information processed on each side to be integrated.

MRI scans are not routinely used in the assessment or diagnosis of straightforward cases of ADHD because the findings above are not in themselves enough upon which to base a diagnosis. Psychiatrists and other doctors might request a MRI scan if they are uncertain of the diagnosis and are looking for other possible causes of the symptoms, for example structural brain damage following a head injury.

During a MRI scan the patient needs to keep still whilst the scanner takes a number of pictures through the head, rather like a series of X-rays. It does not hurt, and most children do not find having the scan unpleasant in any way.

Neurophysiology: Are the Symptoms of ADHD a Reflection of Abnormal Brain Function?

Electroencephalography

A number of studies have been carried out using EEGs (Electroencephalograms). These are traces that represent tiny electrical currents picked up by a number of electrodes attached to the skull, and give clinicians some understanding of the nature of the electrical activity going on in the patient's brain. EEGs are not painful, involving minimal inconvenience and discomfort, and are usually carried out as an outpatient procedure. They are very helpful in establishing whether or not the child has epilepsy, which is relevant when considering treating children with ADHD with certain medications. Epilepsy itself does not usually present with

ADHD-like symptoms, although a few very rare cases have been described. One of the symptoms associated with certain forms of epilepsy and/or its treatment is a reduced attention span. For a more detailed description of this see page 33.

The overall findings drawn from EEG studies in children who have ADHD but no other neurological or psychiatric disorders are rather inconclusive, and it is hard to draw any definite conclusions from them. Several studies have demonstrated a diminished response to stimuli in children with ADHD, but this also occurs in children with other conditions, especially learning disability.

Studies carried out by Drs Buchsbaum and Wender at the National Institute of Mental Health in the USA in 1973 compared the EEG traces of 24 ADHD children with those of 24 non-ADHD children. The EEG traces of the ADHD children had the appearance that one would normally expect in younger children, in that they reflected a less mature pattern of brain electrical activity. Giving the children with ADHD stimulant medication and then repeating the EEGs reduced the differences to the non-ADHD group which were previously observed.

EEGs are not helpful as a diagnostic test for ADHD, but may be requested if the assessing doctor is considering other causes of the symptoms, as several other conditions affecting the brain do have characteristic EEG anomalies.

Blood Flow Studies

Researchers have been able to show that children with ADHD have reduced blood flow to some of the areas of the brain, which are thought to be implicated in the causation of symptoms. These include the Caudate Nucleus (especially in the region of the Striatum) and the frontal areas. These are regions of the brain that have been identified as potentially abnormal in the neuro-anatomical and EEG studies outlined above.

Studies of Metabolic Activity

Positron Emission Tomography (PET) is a technique that has enabled scientists to compare the metabolic activity of certain areas of the brain in people with ADHD with those who do not have ADHD. The technique involves injecting a solution of radioactive glucose into the blood stream. The glucose is taken up by the neurones where it acts as fuel which enables the neurones to function. The proportion of glucose taken up by various areas of the brain is proportional to the level of activity going on in that area. The PET scanning device takes pictures of the brain which demonstrate which areas are most active (those giving off more radioactivity, having taken up more radioactive glucose) and those which are less active.

A number of studies have been carried out in this way with variable results. One such study carried out by Dr Zametkin at the American Institute of Mental Health demonstrated that adolescents and adults with ADHD had reduced metabolic activity in the frontal regions of their brains. This was particularly so on the right side of the brain, and was more pronounced in girls. When people with ADHD were treated with stimulants, the relatively low level of metabolic activity seen in the frontal region was temporarily reversed. These results are very exciting, but we do not know yet whether such findings occur exclusively in ADHD, or if the experiment itself inadvertently demonstrated something else. For example, do the areas of relative metabolic inactivity reflect a state specifically associated with ADHD, or do they merely reflect the consequence of certain types of mental activity carried out by the subjects during the research?

This technique involves the use of radioactive glucose that carries a potential risk to the person being scanned, and the information gleaned from such investigations does not have a direct impact on future treatment or outcome. PET studies are consequently used only as research techniques and are not part of the usual investigation package carried out on people who might have ADHD.

Neurochemistry:
Is ADHD Related to Chemicals in Our Brains?

It seems that ADHD is in some way connected with Dopamine and Noradrenalin (Norepinephrine). These are neurotransmitters, which are chemicals that carry messages between brain cells during mental tasks – rather like the workers moving around and putting things together in a factory.

Medications that act by altering Dopamine and Nor-Adrenaline (Norepinephrine) activity generally improve the symptoms of ADHD. The areas of the brain that are thought to give rise to the symptoms of ADHD have a lot of receptor sites for Dopamine and Noradrenaline. This suggests that these chemicals are involved in the symptoms of ADHD.

Although there have been a lot of research studies that have attempted to explain the chemical basis of the symptoms of ADHD, we do not yet have a coherent explanation of the chemicals and mechanisms involved.

Studies by Zametkin, Shekim *et al.* (1979) and Shen and Wang (1984) demonstrated that children with ADHD have lower levels of the metabolites (waste products) of Noradrenalin (Norepinephrine) in their urine than people who do not have ADHD. Perhaps paradoxically, treatment with stimulant medication increases the levels of these chemicals in the brain, but decreases the concentration of those metabolites in the urine even further.

It seems likely that the neurochemical phenomena behind ADHD are highly complicated, and might well vary between different people with ADHD. It is possible that other neurotransmitters and enzymes are involved in a complex chain of reactions that together explain the causation of the symptoms of ADHD and the therapeutic effect observed when stimulant medications are prescribed.

Dietetics, Toxicology and Allergic Effects

Severe lead poisoning can result in a severe encephalitis in children, and those that recover often show symptoms of inattention and hyperactivity. Children aged 12–36 months are most at risk. Because lead is no longer a component of paint, and lead soldiers have become antiques rather than everyday children's toys, lead poisoning has become increasingly rare.

Exposure to cigarette smoke and alcohol, particularly before birth, may cause damage to children's brains and can result in ADHD-like symptoms. Although there is no conclusive proof that cigarette smoking or alcohol consumption actually causes ADHD, there remains a strong association between these recreational drugs and the disorder. Animal studies have demonstrated that nicotine and alcohol can cause abnormal development of certain brain structures, and it is possible that a similar process occurs in the developing human brain. The symptoms of ADHD are associated with Foetal Alcohol Syndrome, the consequence of excessive alcohol consumption by the child's mother during pregnancy. Other abnormalities of this syndrome include abnormal facial appearance, learning and cognitive difficulties and behavioural problems.

Diet: Is ADHD Related to What the Child Eats?

There has been a lot of interest and speculation about the possibility of diet affecting symptoms of ADHD. Some people have proposed that diets containing additives produce hyperactivity. In particular, yellow food colourings such as the azo-dyes seem to make children hyperactive, and make some children with ADHD excessively hyperactive.

Some special diets been designed to help children with ADHD. One of these diets is the Feingold diet. Sometimes children have been placed on exclusion diets, whereby foods that are thought to cause symptoms are avoided, sometimes resulting in a very limited diet which is not necessarily healthy or nutritious.

There have been some well-designed research projects examining these issues (and also a lot of less well-designed ones). These have demonstrated that some children, particularly atopic children (those vulnerable to eczema, asthma and other allergic conditions) are to some extent sensitive to certain additives.

It must be stressed that excluding additives and other foodstuffs should only be undertaken with professional dietary advice. Dietary measures in themselves are generally not sufficient to alleviate the symptoms of ADHD. If parents have observed that certain foods aggravate their child's symptoms (Smarties and similar sweets are often implicated), it is worth avoiding them. Otherwise current medical opinion is of the belief that dietary change is unlikely to be of much benefit.

Trauma: Are Injuries Responsible for ADHD?

Certain traumas, such as those inflicted by road traffic injuries, encephalitis, and birth trauma can result in ADHD. The brain structures thought to be implicated in the development of ADHD are particularly vulnerable to hypoxic damage during birth (damage resulting from inadequate oxygen reaching parts of the brain whilst blood flow is reduced).

Luk, a Danish researcher, suggested that as the striatum (part of the brain that malfunctions in ADHD) is situated at a watershed in the brain's circulation network, it is at particular risk of being damaged during the birth process, if for any reason the blood supply is reduced (Luk and Leung 1989). This would result in localised hypoxia (reduced oxygen saturation) and would cause permanent damage to the cells affected by causing the release of Glutamate, a powerful neurotoxin.

Contributing Psycho-Social Factors

Sometimes people mistakenly believe that poor or unsatisfactory parenting can result in ADHD. It is important to remember that there is no shortage of evidence that there are many underlying biological mechanisms that are thought to give rise to ADHD. That is not to say that parenting technique does not have an effect on the child's behaviour. The symptoms of ADHD make parenting more difficult. Parents of children with ADHD are sometimes mistakenly accused of being poor or inadequate parents, even if their other children are doing well. Once an effective treatment programme has been implemented, the ADHD symptoms that were thought to be the result of 'poor-parenting' usually evaporate, or at least lessen.

Parenting a child with ADHD is at times extremely tiring and difficult, and families often welcome assistance from professionals to identify anything they do that may inadvertently contribute to their child's symptoms. A child with severe ADHD symptoms is very difficult to parent, and it is likely that some difficulties will have arisen early in life whilst affectionate bonds were being formed. Such difficulties can persist throughout life, and need careful evaluation and appropriate help.

CHAPTER 7

How is the Diagnosis of ADHD Made?

ADHD is considered to be a *spectrum* disorder, in that it seems to exist in varying degrees of severity in different people. It is not easy to distinguish people with mild ADHD from those at the more hyperactive end of 'normal'. Controversy arises from the fact that the diagnosis of ADHD is a difficult one to make. There is no definitive diagnostic test for the disorder, and the symptoms vary according to age and to differing situations and circumstances. The presence of other disorders can obscure the symptoms of ADHD and some of the symptoms of ADHD can occur in other disorders.

People with ADHD have brains that function in a characteristic way, and as a result behave and experience life in a different way from non-ADHD people. To describe them as in some way handicapped is less than helpful. They have a treatable disorder, which when appropriately handled can be well controlled, and they have certain characteristics which, in the right circumstances, can be real strengths. They can become depressed, anxious, or behave in an unacceptable way if undiagnosed or inadequately treated. The most important thing to do is to recognise their underlying symptoms of ADHD, and appreciate how these may take effect.

ADHD always has the same components: impulsiveness, inattention and hyperactivity. It may look different in each child, and even within the same child at different times. It alters depending on what is happening and how the child feels. It may be forgotten or overlooked by adults if something more pressing crops up – for example, if the child with ADHD sets the school on fire or crosses a road without looking, subsequently causing a road traffic accident.

Recognising ADHD is rather like looking into a kaleidoscope: although the pattern you see may vary according to how many turns you make, and it's never the same twice, the pattern is always made of the same components and colours, and reflected through the same number of times.

As soon as they recognise that there is a problem, parents should ask for a medical assessment and should raise the issue of an educational assessment with their child's school. The sooner appropriate treatment and educational interventions are commenced the better. The difficulties associated with ADHD multiply and 'snowball' with time if they are not recognised and dealt with promptly, appropriately and adequately.

In order to ensure that people who may have ADHD receive an accurate diagnosis and appropriate treatment, it is essential that a full and detailed assessment is carried out by a professional who is qualified and experienced enough to do so. ADHD is a medical diagnosis that should be made by a doctor, usually a child and adolescent psychiatrist, a paediatrician or general practitioner. It may well be that ADHD is initially recognised by another professional, such as a teacher or a psychologist, who would then initiate an appropriate referral in order to ensure a full assessment.

Services for children with ADHD and other similar problems are rather patchy in some parts of the UK, and many families find that once they have been referred there is usually some time to wait before an assessment appointment can be offered. Others may have already seen a professional about their child's difficulties, but the question of possible ADHD has not been raised.

If parents are fairly sure that their child does have ADHD but for whatever reason the diagnosis has been missed, it is important to discuss the option of a second opinion with their GP which should be available free of charge on the NHS. Although many families in the recent past have had to seek help from the private sector, often requiring travelling considerable distances, and at their own expense, it should be possible to arrange this within reasonable distance from home and within the NHS. There are a growing number of doctors who recognise ADHD, and are very capable of offering high quality treatment.

A child and adolescent psychiatrist would usually think of looking for symptoms of ADHD when assessing a child referred with behavioural problems. A teacher contending with 30 children, some of whom might be more troublesome and expert in the art of devilment than the child in question, might unwittingly overlook the possibility that he or she has ADHD.

In addition to ensuring that someone meets the diagnostic criteria for ADHD (outlined in the chapter on symptoms of ADHD) it is essential to gain a clear understanding of their personality, their relationships with family and friends, personal strengths and weaknesses, and educational needs. This is crucial when planning appropriate treatment and interventions. There may be other professionals already working with the child and their family. It is extremely important to involve them when designing effective management programmes.

Information Needed for the Assessment of ADHD

A full assessment involves carefully reviewing the child's symptoms and their medical, psychiatric, psychological, educational, personal and family histories. This information is collated with that obtained from reports, interviews by others, clinical observation and examination. When appropriate, professional examinations and assessments from other health professionals and educationalists might be requested. This is time consuming but essential if an accurate assessment of the child's symptoms and needs are to be achieved. There is no single diagnostic test for ADHD and it needs to be distinguished accurately from other psychiatric and psychological disorders. There are no short cuts.

The History of Symptoms and Their Consequences

The doctor will want to consider carefully all the difficulties and symptoms that the child and his or her family are experiencing. They will enquire about the precise nature of such difficulties, including when they were first noticed, the situations in which they occur, factors that exacerbate or relieve them and the effect that they have on the child, and his or her family and friends. They will explore any attempts to deal with the symptoms and how effective such attempts have been. They will be interested in any contact the child and the rest of the family have had with mental health workers or the educational support system.

Medical History

It will be necessary to consider the possible presence of any risk factors that could predispose the child to ADHD. These include difficulties and risks in pregnancy and during birth, including poor maternal health, young age, use of alcohol or smoking, toxaemia or pre-eclampsia (both due to high maternal blood pressure), postmaturity and extended or complicated labour.

The doctor also needs to consider and possibly test for a number of medical conditions known to be associated with ADHD. These are: Fragile X Syndrome, Foetal Alcohol Syndrome, G6PD Deficiency, Phenylketonuria, and Generalised Resistance to Thyroid Hormone. If the doctor has reason to suspect that any of these conditions is present they will order appropriate tests, but as they are all rare conditions it is not necessary routinely to test all children referred.

The doctor will explore other aspects of the child's medical history, including any accidents, operations, and any chronic medical conditions such as epilepsy, asthma, and heart, liver and kidney disorders. They need to know about any prescribed or 'over-the-counter' medications that the child is receiving, and about any allergies or adverse reactions to medication that they might have had in the past.

The doctor needs to consider whether the child has difficulties with their hearing, vision or ability to use and understand speech and language, all of which can have a profound effect on a child's ability to learn, think, form relationships, and behave appropriately. If necessary they will arrange for the child to have an assessment and treatment from an audiologist, an optician or a speech therapist.

Past Psychiatric History

The doctor will enquire about any psychiatric and psychological difficulties that have occurred in the past, and about the effect of any interventions that were made. If necessary, with the parents' consent, they will request copies of any previous assessments and reports. These might be taken into account when reaching a diagnosis and designing a management plan.

Educational History

Because of the impact that ADHD can have on a child's education, social functioning and future career, the doctor will also need to know about the child's experience of the education system to date. This needs to include their academic progress, the level of their ability and the nature of any specific difficulties, their ability to function as part of their peer group, how they get on with teachers and other people in authority, and any difficulties encountered regarding behaviour and possible suspensions and exclusions. The doctor, again with the parents' consent, will wish to contact the child's school, to request oral and/or written reports. If necessary, the doctor and the child's teachers will discuss the potential need for an educational psychologist's assessment, assistance from the behavioural support service or special educational needs teachers, and any assistance the doctor needs from the teachers in the assessment and treatment of the child. This process will form the basis of what is potentially a crucial therapeutic alliance between the school and health service. In some areas the assistance of the school nurses and doctors will be sought at this point.

Assessment of the Child and Parents' Temperament, Personalities, Relationships and Social Circumstances

A very important part of the assessment will involve exploring the child's temperament and personality, those of other family members and the nature of relationships within the immediate and extended family. The doctor will wish to discuss the techniques that the parents have used in attempts to address their child's difficulties, and how effective these have been.

Although this might perhaps seem intrusive, it is of paramount importance because such issues can have a profound effect on the way a child (and parents) think, feel and behave. The assessing doctor should try to undertake this in an unthreatening manner, and not attribute blame to any one family member. For the sake of both child and parents the doctor will attempt to remain neutral, and should give careful consideration to who is present for each part of the discussion. For example, it is not helpful to a child to see embittered arguing parents who are trying to cope with traumatic divorce proceedings, each trying to get the doctor to see the situation, the cause of the child's difficulties, and possible solutions, from their own point of view.

Family History

The doctor will also consider the mental and medical health of the child's parents and other family members, enquiring about the presence of conditions such as ADHD or depression. This is relevant both in understanding the origin of the child's difficulties and also when planning effective interventions.

Social Assessment

A general assessment of the family's social circumstances needs to be made, with particular reference to:

- ° Housing (e.g. the effects of overcrowding; living in a high-rise flat with nowhere for the child to run about and expend their energies; living in an area where illicit drug use and violence abound).

° Parents' employment, unemployment and child care arrangements.

° Social support, and contact between different family members.

° Interaction between the child and other members of the community, for example, youth clubs, parent and toddler groups.

° The presence or absence of financial worries, and the parent's awareness of any benefits or social support that they and their child might qualify for.

° Any difficulties or pressures the family might be experiencing that could have an impact on the child.

° Whether or not social services are involved, and how they might be able to help the child and their family.

When appropriate the doctor will liaise with social services regarding their assessment of the child and potential therapeutic social interventions, and might suggest that the parents approach them or the Benefits Agency for help.

Information from Other Professionals

The doctor may request assessments from other professionals if necessary. These might include assessments by an educational psychologist (e.g. to see if the child has Specific Learning Disabilities, Dyslexia, or any other psychological abnormality that may be relevant to the diagnosis or their education), or a speech and language therapist.

Forensic History

Any contact with the police or criminal justice system (when relevant) also needs to be considered.

Physical Examination and Investigations

The doctor will carry out a physical examination of the child, looking for any abnormalities that might be relevant to either the diagnosis or treatment. In particular, they will look for signs of neurological abnormalities (such as clumsiness or co-ordination problems (dyspraxia), signs of motor tic disorders or Gilles de la Tourette's Syndrome) and for evidence of any heart or circulation, kidney or liver disease that could have implications for medical treatment.

Investigations

Observation of the Child

An important part of the assessment of the child will include careful observation of the child. This will form an important part of the doctor's initial assessment, and he or she will observe the child's behaviour and interactions with others during the consultation. On occasions observations may be carried out in school or other settings, for example as part of an educational psychologist's assessment in the classroom. Care needs to be taken to ensure that 'observer bias' is not inadvertently brought into the equation if the child or their classmates recognise that the observation is taking place and consequently alter their behaviour. Potentially, observation is helpful not only in making a diagnosis and understanding the nature of the relationships the child forms with others, but also in providing the information that forms the basis of future educational, psychotherapeutic and social skills interventions.

Blood Tests

If indicated the doctor will order appropriate tests for the conditions outlined above that might be of relevance to the diagnosis or management plan. These might also include Chromosome Analysis if Fragile X Syndrome, or other conditions associated with chromosomal abnormalities, is suspected; or

Thyroid Function Tests if there are signs of hypothyroidism. Usually such tests are not indicated.

Other Neurological Investigations

If the doctor has reason to suspect that the child has a demonstrable neurological problem, he or she might order an EEG (Electroencephalogram) or a brain scan, such as an MRI or CAT scan. These scans show the structure of the brain and any structural abnormalities. The results are rather like x-rays to look at – the films show black-and-white cross-sections of the area scanned. Both types of scan are relatively straightforward, painless investigations, carried out in the local hospital radiology department. The patient keeps his or her head very still while the scanner takes its pictures. The doctor may need to look for evidence of epilepsy or of brain damage caused during labour or as a result of a head injury. These techniques are not part of the assessment of relatively straightforward ADHD.

Rating Scales

Behavioural Rating Scales

There are a number of Behavioural Rating Scales that have been developed and validated (checked to see that they really do demonstrate what they set out to do). Some of the most useful are included in Appendix I to this book. These can be very helpful both in the initial assessment of ADHD and during on-going treatment as measures of the effectiveness of interventions that have been implemented. Some of these rating scales relate specifically to ADHD – such as the symptom checklists designed by Rutter (1967) and Du Paul (1991) – and some of them are more general. In order to establish whether or not the child displays symptoms of ADHD in both at home and at school, the Barkley Home Situation and School Situation Questionnaires can be very helpful. These later questionnaires can be found as part of a very detailed and comprehensive assessment package described by

Gordon (1995), which would be of interest to doctors working in ADHD clinics.

The behavioural rating scales scores are very vulnerable to distortion, because they depend on the subjective view that person filling them in has of the child. Misleading conclusions can be drawn if they are filled in by an angry and disheartened or even rejecting parent; or by a teacher who does not believe in the concept of ADHD and has a differing view regarding the nature and cause of the child's difficulties; or simply by someone who doesn't know the child very well or only has contact with the child in highly structured settings (such as a psychiatric in-patient therapeutic community). See Appendix I for more information.

Screening More Generally for Emotional and Behavioural Disturbances

There are other checklists that apply more generally, because they screen for a wide variety of emotional and behavioural symptoms and difficulties that occur in childhood and adolescence. Some of the more commonly used ones include: The Child Behaviour Checklist, Teacher Report Form, and Youth Self-Report Form designed by Professor Achenbach; the Conner's Questionnaires for parents and teachers, and the Strengths and Weaknesses Questionnaire, designed by Professor Goodman. These rating scales give the doctor a wider view of the child's functional level, and may indicate that additional or alternative diagnoses need to be considered.

Continuous Performance Tests

A number of attempts have been made to design an instrument that gives a more objective measurement of the nature and severity of the child's ADHD symptoms than the behavioural rating scales. Continuous performance tests – for example, the Gordon Diagnostic System – attempt to remove the subjective element and measure the child's difficulties in a way that is independent of the relationship between the child and their assessor. They attempt, therefore, to measure the abnormal biological and psychological aspect of the child's functioning. The Gordon Diagnostic System is built as a computer game that attempts to measure the child's impulse control, distractibility and vigilance. It is impossible to design a 'pure' test that only measures these parameters, and the continuous performance tests have been criticised because motivation, determination and high intelligence can distort the results. (For more information see Appendix I to this book.) Such tests do not accurately identify all those who have and do not have ADHD, but when also taking into account all the other information gathered in the course of an ADHD assessment, many clinicians find them to be extremely useful and informative.

The assessing doctor will collect all this information, perhaps over several assessment appointments, before drawing their conclusions together and making a diagnosis. In addition to establishing whether or not the child has ADHD, they will consider the possible existence of other psychiatric, psychological, neuropsychiatric or behavioural conditions. They will take into account the presence, severity and nature of any learning disabilities, medical conditions and any relationship or social difficulties that the child and his or her family might be encountering.

It is only when the doctor, the child and the parents have discussed this, and agreed on the precise nature and severity of the difficulties in question, that an effective treatment plan can be designed and implemented.

Although there are a lot of questions to be answered, it is essential that they are given due consideration. It is only once the doctor has an accurate idea of both the nature and causes of the child's difficulties that he or she can design an appropriate management plan that will work.

Assessment Of ADHD

History of the child's difficulties

Medical and psychiatric history

Physical examination

Other information (school, educational psychology, speech and language, audiologist and optician)

Investigations

Rating Scales (Conner's, Du Paul, Child Behaviour Checklist etc)

Continuous performance tests (Gordon Diagnostic System)

CHAPTER 8

The Treatment Team

The good news is that almost all the symptoms and difficulties experienced by people with ADHD are potentially treatable. Several very successful and famous people are alleged to have had ADHD, including Sir Winston Churchill and J.F. Kennedy. It is essential to find a treatment programme that works. Just as the assessment requires the help of many people, the management plan will also need a 'Team' approach.

Educational Psychologists

Educational psychologists are trained in psychology and have particular expertise in the areas where psychology interacts with education. They can become involved with a number of tasks:

° Testing the children to establish their abilities and difficulties, including IQ testing

° Advising the school on how best to assist the child

° Counselling the child

° Acting as key expert in the statementing procedures.

Behavioural Support Services

There are teachers and teaching assistants employed by each local authority to support schools. They can give practical advice on how to deal with behavioural problems in children and adolescents, and have particular skills in helping children who find learning difficult.

Different education authorities have different names for these services, and the child's school usually accesses them, when it is felt to be appropriate, having tried alternative approaches to the child's difficulties themselves. These services can often provide advice to class teachers, or on occasions teach the child in the school itself.

Some behavioural support services also include special units, often referred to as pupil referral units, which operate along the lines of small schools specialising in behavioural and learning difficulties. They may accept the child for a limited length of time in order to assess their needs and go some way to addressing these, before reintegrating the child into an appropriate mainstream school with any necessary support.

School Nurses and Doctors

School nurses, and in some areas, school doctors, are often the first 'port of call' for teachers and parents who have concerns about a child or young person's physical or mental health. They will be familiar with the sorts of conditions that affect young people, and will be able to assist parents in finding out who to seek help from, and how the local referral procedures work. It may well be that it is the school nurse or doctor who first suspects that the child has ADHD. They have provided us with invaluable assistance in ensuring that our patients receive their medication at school (not always as easy as it sounds) and in supporting and counselling children in school.

In some areas, school nurses and doctors are becoming increasingly involved in the diagnosis and treatment of disorders such as ADHD, working hand-in-hand with child and adolescent psychiatrists, paediatricians, and educational psychologists.

Social Services

Although just the mention of social services seems to worry many families, especially those who are experiencing difficulties with their children, many families have found their help invaluable. They can be of particular help in accessing many 'Godsends'.

They may be able to find the child a place on school holiday activity programmes, improving their social life and self-esteem, relieving holiday boredom and keeping them out of trouble, whilst giving parents a break. They can also access local facilities appropriate to the child's needs.

Some families may be entitled to Disability Living Allowances and other benefits. Social workers are particularly skilled in dealing with the DHSS. Many social workers offer considerable support to families in difficulty, and can also introduce the child to their own support worker where appropriate. They are also essential in cases where, for whatever reason, a child could be at risk or needs to go into care.

Psychologists

Psychologists, unlike medical doctors (general practitioners, psychiatrists and paediatricians), do not prescribe medication to treat physical illnesses. They are highly trained professionals who have particular expertise in the non-drug management of psychiatric and psychological difficulties. They can offer a great deal of help and advice to children and families living with ADHD, and in many instances will be the mainstay of treatment. They can work with children alone, with parents or families, and work using a variety of techniques on thoughts, feelings, behaviour, self-confidence and social skills, and also can offer constructive help when relationships are not as good as they should be.

Unfortunately, like child and adolescent psychiatrists, child psychologists are rather thin on the ground in parts of this country. The good news is that there are overlaps in the training of doctors, psychologists, nurses and teachers, and it will usually be possible to find someone who can provide this essential help.

Family Therapists

Family therapists have usually trained as nurses, psychologists, social workers, doctors or in one of the allied professions, and gained practical experience of working with families, before undertaking additional training in family therapy. Because mental health problems in children can take such a heavy toll on families and because the child's 'problem' is in reality likely to be a problem that affects the whole family and 'belongs' to everyone, family therapists are essential members of most Children's Mental Health teams. As ADHD can have such far reaching and potentially damaging effects on families, family therapy in some shape or form can offer distinct advantages to many people.

The therapist will probably assume a 'position of neutrality', which means that they do not side with any one family member, and try to enable the family members to speak in a safe and unthreatening environment. The idea is not to tell families what to do or to judge them in any way, but to enable them to communicate clearly, and devise their own solutions to the difficulties they are facing.

The Extended Family and Voluntary Agencies

Many families living with a child with ADHD find that the help that their extended family is able to offer them, both practical, and in terms of moral support, is of enormous importance. Some parents are initially very cautious about asking for help, often because they think that other family members have judged them to be poor parents. We see many families who have other children who do not have ADHD and who are quite different from their affected sibling. They are the living proof that perfectly competent parents can find parenting a child with ADHD extremely difficult.

Often, once a diagnosis has been made, and effective treatment started, other family members will start to see that the child with ADHD and his parents are all in fact the victims of a treatable disorder. Helping relatives to understand more about ADHD will enable them to 'say and do the right thing', when attempting to help. Giving or showing them information, a parents' handbook or video, or even taking them along to a lecture or parents' support group may do the trick.

Similarly, a football coach or guide leader, who understands the nature of ADHD, could offer the child that crucial chance to excel at something, make rewarding friendships with children who haven't given up on them already, and develop the confidence and self-esteem that we all need so much. Again, parents may have to educate them a bit, and persuade them to give their child an opportunity to succeed.

The Parent Support Groups

There are currently several parent support groups, many of them operating independently, often affiliated to one or more of the main national groups. Some of the addresses can be found at the end of this book.

There may be groups within driving distance that hold lectures by internationally renowned speakers to their members. These are usually open to all interested families. Family support groups often know their way around their local health and education authorities, and departments of social services. This knowledge can save parents of newly diagnosed children, or those who can't seem to get effective help, a great deal of legwork and unnecessary worry. Some of them also seem to be able to assist parents in obtaining benefits to which they are entitled, but which the DHSS has previously kept thinking of reasons to refuse.

At a national level, these groups are working very hard to put ADHD firmly onto the political agenda, and hold large conferences and meetings, open to professionals and parents. They aim to increase awareness of ADHD and related conditions, and to improve the quality of interventions offered to young people with ADHD and their families.

Because ADHD is being increasingly recognised and diagnosed, there are enormous implications for public spending. The Treasury is unlikely to be willing or able to part with the enormous sums of money that would be required to set up effective multi-agency services for ADHD (remember that at present we are only aware of and treating about 1 in 10 of affected children).

There is no acceptable reason for this group of children to be denied the treatment and help they require, but we shall all, professionals, parents and young people, have to work together to ensure that they do not get overlooked amongst a multitude of worthy groups. For further information, see Appendix II.

The ADHD Treatment Team
The child and his or her family
The assessing doctor
Family GP
School teacher
Educational psychologists
Behavioural support system
School nurse and doctor
Social services
Psychologists
Family therapists
The extended family and voluntary agencies
Parents' support groups

CHAPTER 9

Medical Treatment

There are many treatments and interventions that can be used to help people with ADHD. These include: medication, psychological treatments, educational interventions and social interventions. These are described in detail in the following chapters.

For children with moderate to severe ADHD medication can make a real difference to behaviour, thinking and learning ability, and their relationships with others. In some cases, it is only when a child is on appropriate medication that other interventions start to take effect.

In those children with milder symptoms it may be more appropriate to consider using a combination of psychological, social and educational approaches first.

In each case, the decision to prescribe must be made by the doctor in collaboration with the young person concerned and his or her parents. Doctors may occasionally be wrong in their initial treatment decision. If the outcome following treatment does not prove to be effective, they should be open to the suggestions and requests of others involved with the child in question and try different interventions.

If medication is prescribed, it is vital for the prescribing doctor to talk to the child and to explain fully the reason why he or she should start on medication. Many children will want to ask questions or discuss any fears they have concerning this. Some children may believe that they have been prescribed medication for being naughty. In those cases they may see medication as a punishment and not as something that can be helpful to them. The child's opinion should be listened to, when considering the prescription of any medication. For more detailed descriptions of medications see Rosenberg *et al.* (1994) and Spencer *et al.* (1996).

The main drug types available in Britain at present include:

Stimulants

In Britain the most effective and frequently used medications are stimulants, mainly Methylphenidate (Ritalin) and Dexamphentamine (Dexadrine). These medications are derivatives from Amphetamine and when correctly used are very safe and effective drugs.

Ritalin

It has been known since 1937 that ADHD and related conditions respond to stimulant medication. There is an art to setting the dose right, in order to gain maximum benefit without side effects, and it usually takes a while to get it just right.

Prescribing in the UK is a relatively rare occurrence, in contrast to the USA where there has been a dramatic increase in prescribing stimulants, in some classrooms up to 5 or 10 per cent of children being on stimulant medication, giving rise to concern. If anything, in the UK we are under-diagnosing and under-prescribing, and consequently depriving many children of appropriate treatment, and an effective education, not to mention the human cost of strained and battered relationships.

Recent figures suggest that only one child in ten with ADHD is receiving appropriate medication in the UK.

WHAT ARE THE EFFECTS OF RITALIN?

Ritalin reduces hyperactivity and impulsiveness, and increases attention span. With these effects, things start to improve in other ways for the child and their family, in that the child tends to have greater control over their impulses. They become less aggressive and seem to listen to and comply with requests and commands. They make fewer mistakes as they start to hear and register requests. They become less forgetful. Their abilities at school often improve dramatically; for some children this is partly effected by no longer getting sent out of class or sent home. The quality of their work improves, and presentation and literacy skills get better. As they are no longer irritating, frustrating or worrying people who are important to them, children often become much happier and more willing to try. They are no longer in trouble all the time, and their self-confidence improves in parallel with their self control.

After an initial 'honeymoon' period of dramatic improvement and understandable relief to all concerned, the full extent of the damage wreaked by the ADHD becomes apparent, and the long slow process of learning how to do all the things that were difficult or impossible before commences. Skills that most of us learn without realising, such as how to make friends, or how to develop a hobby or interest, may now become a major learning task for the child with ADHD.

The child whose social position depended on him being the class fool, now has to discover a new social niche. This may involve making new friends. Relationships must heal and be renegotiated at home. There may be enormous levels of anger and regret, as well as resentment towards those who identified the cause of previous difficulties to the child's temperament or to 'poor parenting'.

In the months that follow the introduction of effective treatment, children start to make very noticeable improvements in their academic work. This may involve catching up with their peers, whilst others, who have in fact, been under-performing will start to excel, and surprise everyone with their abilities.

All this may sound too good to be true, yet time and time again dramatic improvements occur when a child is adequately treated. The downside of medication is that the child has tablets to take on a very regular basis, and practical and emotional issues relating to this must be addressed.

HOW DOES RITALIN WORK?

It has been suggested that the brains of people with ADHD are 'set' differently from those of other people, in that the areas of their brains that maintain alertness and arousal require higher levels of stimulation to remain alert and maintain concentration and attention. The medication effectively resets their brain. It has even been suggested that people with ADHD actively behave in a way that keeps them awake, which begins to explain why the rest of us find them so disruptive and irritatingly noisy at times.

Ritalin probably exerts its beneficial effects on ADHD by increasing the number of chemical messengers (neurotransmitters) particularly Dopamine and Nor-adrenaline, in the tiny gaps between brain cells (the synaptic clefts).

HOW MUCH MEDICATION DOES THE CHILD NEED?

The doctor will probably prescribe in multiples of 5mg (= ½ a 10mg tablet), starting at a low dose and gradually moving upwards, until the dose that gives maximum advantage without side effects is found. To ensure that the child gets the correct dose, the pharmacist will probably cut the tablets in half. Alternatively the doctor could ask them to provide a tablet cutter. The maximum dose that is recommended in the UK is 60mg/24hrs. Most children do not need that much.

HOW OFTEN SHOULD THE TABLETS BE TAKEN?

Ritalin is absorbed from the stomach within about half an hour of taking it. It will reach its highest concentration in the brain within an hour or two, and will cease to act after about four or five hours as it is quickly metabolised and excreted. The tablets will need to be given regularly, carefully spacing them at approximately four-hour intervals. The precise timing will need to be carefully worked out, taking into account the rate at which the child appears to metabolise his tablets, and the situations he will find himself in, as well as when it is possible to administer the tablets in school.

Many children find that it is a good idea to take the first dose when they wake up in the morning. This means that medication will take effect in time to ensure that they have a little 'quality time' at home (aiding the process of relationship-healing), before they venture out into the traffic and the playground. Remember that these children are much less able to cope with unstructured times than with structured orderly ones. Timing in this way should help them start the day 'on a good note', and ensure that they enjoy some sort of social life before the work of the day commences.

The timing of the second dose depends on how long the first lasts. The blood and brain levels required to control behaviour are not always the same as those to ensure effective thinking or learning, so the observations of teachers become absolutely essential. It may be prudent to give the second dose at break time, if the effects are wearing off, although many children will make it through to mid-day. Enough should be given to ensure that the child both learns and stays out of trouble all day. That includes lunch hour, and the journey home on the school bus, times at which so many ADHD children seem to get into so much trouble. It is important that the child and the family experience time together when medication has effectively controlled the ADHD symptoms.

Ritalin can be taken with or without food, although many children will prefer, at least initially, to take it with a spoon of ice cream or jam, or some other 'tooth-rotting-but-sweet-and-yummy substance'. Dentists may cringe, but this is a useful way of getting the 'essential substance' into a stroppy and oppositional (probably frightened) child. Some children say that Ritalin tastes nasty, unless quickly swallowed. The aim is to do good, and certainly no harm, so maybe the timing of tooth brushing could be altered.

Once the correct dose has been established, the GP should be able to take over routine prescribing of Ritalin. Most GPs are not sufficiently trained or experienced in altering the dose according to need, so the child and adolescent psychiatrist or paediatrician will see the child every few months to monitor progress and needs, after appropriate psychological and other interventions have been set up. They will communicate and liaise with the GP.

Ritalin is a controlled drug. It has to be prescribed in a very precise way. The pharmacist may well want to check before issuing this medication, particularly if they do not know the child's family or work in an area where there is a lot of drug abuse. It is wise to get the prescription dispensed at the same pharmacy each time.

All medication should be kept locked up, and out of the way of children and confused people. A sensible adult should supervise its use, although it is a good idea to involve children, particular in remembering when it is due. Teenagers who can be relied upon to act responsibly may be allowed to take more control, as long as it remains safely locked up, and the prescribed dose is adhered to. Schools will need to make special arrangements as it is not desirable, nor is it allowed to have such medications in the child or young person's possession.

DOES RITALIN PRODUCE ADDICTION?

There is no evidence to suggest that when used appropriately, even for years, in the treatment of ADHD, addiction or drug dependence will develop. Ritalin is an Amphetamine derivative, and could be subject to abuse if special precautions are not taken. It is a medication with a potential street value and must not find its way into unscrupulous hands.

Doctors carefully record exactly how much medication they have prescribed for each child, and its effects are monitored by several members of the core team, to prevent inappropriate amounts being dispensed.

OTHER IMPORTANT INFORMATION

The prescribing doctor must remain in charge of the dose of any medication used to treat ADHD. The dose must only be altered with their permission. Contrary to some misguided or maybe desperate people's belief, more is not always, or even nearly always, best! There are often serious problems and side effects associated with high levels of stimulants, especially when the concentration of the medication in the blood falls. For this reason the dose needs to be carefully adjusted and spaced to give maximum advantage. If there are persisting difficulties the doctor will need to think very carefully about what and how to prescribe.

Parents should not follow the advice of anybody but the child's doctor and qualified pharmacist. If they think that the prescription needs to be altered in any way they should discuss this with the prescribing doctor.

WHAT ARE THE SIDE EFFECTS OF RITALIN AND OTHER STIMULANTS?

° *Insomnia:* The child may not fall asleep until much later than usually. This can occur when the last dose is given too late. The last dose should usually be given before 4pm to prevent rebound effects that can occur if blood levels fall too rapidly. There are various ways around this difficulty. If insomnia does become a problem, it is wise to tell the prescribing doctor about it before every one in the family gets completely exhausted.

° *Appetite loss:* Stimulants have also been used to help people lose weight by reducing appetite. This is not the intention in treating a growing child for ADHD. Some families get round this side effect by ensuring that the child has a big breakfast before his tablet, and feeding him more in the evening. Parents may well have to take more 'control' of the child's appetite than they would normally. Doctors deliberately monitor children's height and weight to keep an eye on this. Despite previous concerns, there is good evidence that Ritalin does not stop children growing. It seems that the 'growth delay' observed in children on stimulants is actually related to the developmental delay that is a part of ADHD itself, and not a side effect of stimulants. It is important to note that any child who is unhappy or not eating sufficiently will not grow as well as may be expected.

° *Less frequent side effects:* Some children can get tics, become irritable or even depressed. They may also complain of tummy pains, headaches, feeling sick, dizziness, dry mouth or constipation. These side effects are usually seen at higher doses, when trying to get maximum benefit from the tablets. Of course, Ritalin is not the only cause of these symptoms, so they should be discussed with the child's GP, child and adolescent psychiatrist or paediatrician so that they can decide what is wrong and what to do. These symptoms usually resolve when the dose is reduced, particularly if Ritalin has caused the side-effects in the first place.

It is usually recommended that children on Ritalin have six-monthly blood counts, and their height, weight, and blood pressure measured. GPs should be able to arrange this close to home.

HOW LONG SHOULD CHILDREN WITH ADHD TAKE MEDICATION?

Many children with ADHD will 'grow out' of their disorder, or at least the symptoms may become easier to control, and the young person will have managed to acquire various skills to assist themselves. In practice, a younger child is probably going to need treatment for some time, possibly years.

It is good practice to stop medication for a week or two, perhaps at yearly intervals, to see how the child is able to cope. This should always be a planned exercise, undertaken with the help of the prescribing doctor, and the teachers, at a time of year that will clearly demonstrate how behaviour and learning ability are affected, without jeopardising the child's chance of success in examinations or other important events.

In the past doctors recommended that stimulant medication should be regularly stopped at weekends and during school holidays in order to let the child 'catch up' with growth, which was believed to be slowed by the treatment. Current thinking suggests that this apparent 'slowing of growth' has nothing to do with the tablets at all – rather, it is thought to be part of a developmental delay that is due to the underlying ADHD itself. We normally recommend that with the exception of the planned breaks in treatment (to see if it is still needed), children should receive appropriate treatment every day. Children with ADHD have more to learn than schoolwork. There is so much to be enjoyed and learnt in life, including getting on with your family and friends, and being able to safely participate fully in all the opportunities life offers.

It is becoming apparent that some people with ADHD will not grow out of their symptoms, and will continue to need their prescriptions. This is a need that one way or another the health service will have to meet in the near future. Adequate adult services will need to take on the 'ADHD Graduates' of the child and adolescent psychiatrists and paediatricians.

Dexadrine (Dexamphetamine)

For financial reasons, this is the most commonly used drug for ADHD in Australia. It is used somewhat less in the UK, but is nonetheless an effective and useful medication.

From a pharmacological point of view it is chemically related to Ritalin, is an Amphetamine, a controlled drug, and exerts its effect on ADHD in much the same way.

It does not offer any distinct advantage or disadvantage over Ritalin, but it may prove effective in children who do not respond to Ritalin. It has a 'longer life' in the bloodstream and brain, so it could be of use in reducing the need to administer medication so frequently. It has similar side effects to Ritalin.

Tricyclic Antidepressants

Imipramine

About 30 per cent of children with ADHD treated with stimulants will not experience effective symptom relief. Children with significant anxiety or depressive symptoms in addition to ADHD are particularly likely to fail to respond to stimulants, and their symptoms may actually worsen.

There is a great deal of evidence to suggest that some of the Tricyclic Antidepressants are effective in reducing the core symptoms of ADHD, although not as effectively as the stimulants do when they work. They improve mood and hyperactivity, but as they also have sedative properties, do not improve learning.

This medication can be very helpful to some children, particularly those who have ADHD plus anxiety or depression as well. They can be used to 'kill two birds with one stone' as they reduce the symptoms of ADHD, anxiety and depression.

The risk of not treating ADHD effectively must be taken into account when considering the use of these drugs. Depressed children may attempt suicide, and are not able to learn, socialise, or feel happy. An anxious child may be so anxious that they are not able to function normally. It is well known that ADHD children are involved in more accidents, and could sustain a serious injury if not adequately treated.

This medication is not metabolised as quickly as stimulants, and therefore can be given as a single dose at bedtime, yet take effect all day.

SIDE EFFECTS

Secondary effects of the medication can include dry mouth, constipation, rashes, raised blood pressure, confusion, seizures, and abnormal heart rhythms, amongst other things. In practice, only the first two symptoms are usually seen, if any, and thousands of children take them without any difficulty.

There have been a small number of case reports describing sudden death in children taking Desipramine (which is chemically very similar to Imipramine). These mostly occurred in children who had taken either accidental or deliberate overdoses of medication. There are some concerns that on very rare occasions children who had been taking a recommended dose of Desipramine for some time and who had not taken an overdose also died suddenly. The reason for this is not clear.

Most doctors both in the UK and in the USA would consider using Tricyclic Antidepressants when other safer options have not worked, and there are no clear contraindications in the child in question.

OTHER IMPORTANT INFORMATION

Certain precautions need to be taken when prescribing Tricyclic Antidepressants for children, including recording an ECG (heart trace) before and during treatment, and also checking the child's blood pressure and pulse regularly and accurately. The help of a paediatrician should be sought immediately, if there is cause for concern. For further information see Rosenberg *et al.* (1994).

Antipsychotic Medications

Haloperidol and Chlorpromazine

By 1996 there had been about 12 studies including 242 children and adolescents evaluating the effectiveness and safety of antipsychotic medication for ADHD.

THE EFFECTIVE DOSE

In the studies, the effective dose varied widely, with similar results obtained from low doses and high ones. Not more than 50 per cent of patients responded and two thirds of the studies showed them to be less effective than stimulants.

SIDE EFFECTS

It is believed that one in eight children treated with these drugs could develop Tardive Dyskinesia, a very disabling movement disorder that is exceptionally difficult to treat. Other side effects include stiffness and tremor of the limbs, sedation, dry mouth and constipation.

For these reasons, and because there are safer and more effective treatments available, these drugs are not usually used for ADHD. There are, however other conditions in which these drugs have an important role, and sensitivity to side effects diminishes with age (at least until old age).

There has recently been some interest in the potential benefits from Risperidone, a new antipsychotic drug that is less likely to produce serious side effects and some parents have considered acquiring it for their ADHD children.

Antihypertensives

Clonidine

This medication is used with some success in some children with ADHD. It is often used later in the day to provide symptom control without the insomnia that late use of stimulants often causes. It is a treatment that offers promise in the treatment of ADHD occurring with tics or Gilles de la Tourette's Syndrome, when occasionally stimulants are believed to increase motor tics.

Possible side effects include dry mouth, sedation, nausea, dizziness and occasional rashes. It should be used with caution in patients with depression.

Propranolol

Drugs of this class are sometimes used to treat anxiety and temper/aggressive outbursts in adult psychiatry, so perhaps it is not so surprising that people with ADHD should gain some relief of psychological symptoms. There are no reports to date of it being used in children.

Drug Combinations

When a child partially responds to medication, but still has symptoms that are troublesome, and/or has another condition existing with their ADHD, it is sometimes possible to achieve better symptom relief by using two medications together.

An example of this would be a teenager with significant ADHD in addition to a depressive illness, who has been treated initially with a Tricyclic Antidepressant at an adequate dose, for a sufficiently long time. The depressive symptoms have been relieved, but troublesome ADHD symptoms remain. One possible solution for this would be to add Ritalin to treat the underlying ADHD and to continue the antidepressant to treat the depression.

Another option would be to persist with the Tricyclic and explore alternative strategies for coping with the ADHD symptoms, for example educational and behavioural interventions. This option may spare the teenager from the increase in symptoms that can occur in some young people who have ADHD and depressive and/or anxiety symptoms and who are treated with stimulants.

There is a possibility of interactions between drugs, for example between anti-psychotic medication and antidepressants, or between stimulants and Imipramine. Because of this the assessment and treatment of more complicated cases of ADHD are usually best dealt with by a child and adolescent psychiatrist with experience in the management of more complex cases, and poly-pharmacy. There will usually be a consultant within travelling distance who will be able to deal with such cases. The advantage of seeing a child and adolescent psychiatrist as opposed to another type of doctor, is that they are specifically trained to be able to recognise the need for, and instigate a whole range of psychological and drug therapies, often using a combination of the two. There is real art to psychiatry, in addition to the optimal management of ADHD, and as time is 'of the essence' when treating mental health problems in young people we would strongly recommend that parents enlist the help of their GP in obtaining the best possible help for their child.

Medications for the Future

We hope that there will soon be some safer, more convenient, and effective medications for ADHD. One product type, already available in the USA is slow-release Methylphenidate (Ritalin) and Dexamphetamine (Dexadrine). These forms of the most commonly used treatments slowly release the medication once it has been swallowed over a few hours. It is argued that the advantage of this is that it is not necessary to give the tablets so frequently (because they last longer), and they can give smoother and better symptom control. Other trials have shown that better symptom control is obtained with the original, non-slow-release form of the drug.

There is always the possibility that drugs already tried and tested for other disorders will be found to have a use in the treatment of ADHD. One example of this is Guanfacine, an antihypertensive drug, similar to Clonidine, which is currently under review in the USA.

Although it takes many years to identify, develop and market new medicines, not least when they are largely intended for children, it is believed that the drug industry is in the process of developing exciting new treatments. These are likely to be based on our ever-increasing knowledge of the neuroscience that may, in a few years' time offer great help to people with ADHD.

Medication often has a dramatic and far-reaching effect, apparently miraculously resolving all those troublesome symptoms and behaviours, improving learning ability and social functioning in many cases. It is essential to remember that the tablets are not a cure; that they temporarily 'normalise' brain function and the way a child thinks, feels and behaves. Until the young person learns new ways to control his or her impulses and to focus attention sufficiently on the task in hand, they should be regarded as a crutch, not the cure.

Medication for ADHD	Type	Dose	Side effects
Ritalin	Stimulant	5–60mg	Insomnia Appetite Loss Tics
Dexamphetamine	Stimulant	5–20mg	Same as above
Tricyclics (e.g. Imipramine)	Anti-depressant	Up to 5mg/kg /day	Dry mouth Constipation Seizures
Haloperidol Chlorpromazine	Anti-psychotic	Low doses	Movement disorders Tremor Dry mouth Tardive dyskinesia
Clonidine Propranolol	Anti-hypertensive		Dry mouth Nausea Sedation

CHAPTER 10

Psychological Treatments

The answer to the difficulties encountered by young people with the symptoms of ADHD and their families does not lie exclusively in a pillbox.

People with ADHD have additional difficulties that can potentially cause serious problems to other people, but they are in all other respects normal people. They have thoughts, feeling, hopes, and dreams like anyone else. One real risk of 'obtaining a diagnosis', which is clearly a priority for many families living with a child with unrecognised ADHD, is that once obtained, the child is often seen purely in terms of their diagnosis and the consequences of their neurological difficulties. Children with difficulties and disabilities of all sorts are first and foremost children, not disorders or syndromes.

If we are effectively to help the child to feel and to function in a more appropriate and rewarding way it is imperative that we consider what it feels like to be that child. How does it feel to be told you have a disorder, but (all too often) not what that entails, or the positive side of it all? What does it feel like to realise that all along you have been different from everyone else in some indefinable way, and for that realisation to be formally recognised? How does it feel when every time you really try things go wrong and 'blow up in your face'? You try to learn, to be good, and to make friends, but your head lets you down, and you 'blow it' nearly every time? What on earth have you been called, accused of, and experienced in the past? Will this diagnosis, the treatment and the professionals that you have to see make life better or worse? Will the other children call you names and reject you further, or will they help and encourage you, invite you to their parties, to join in their games, now that you seem to have some degree of control over yourself?

In order really to help these children all these questions and issues must be considered and addressed. It will take a lot of imagination, good will and effort from all involved. Similarly, it is important to address similar issues for the family and the professionals who have been trying so hard, for so long, often with little success.

Many of the mothers we work with describe the humiliation of being constantly called to school to 'do something' with a child that no-one can do anything with; of suspecting, or knowing that professionals and others think that you are an incompetent or 'bad' parent.

This can be heightened when professional people who see the child for limited lengths of time, often on a one-to-one basis, in a quiet or highly structured environment, proclaim that as they have less difficulty with the child, there is clearly something wrong with 'the parenting'!

Such parents may have a child, maybe children, that no-one wants to play with or help with, and possibly other children who are suffering as a consequence of their sibling's difficulties. Fathers also experience these things. What sort of parent could live with all this without feeling despair, fear, humiliation, and defeat?

Teachers and social workers may similarly feel humiliated, frustrated, or be accused of incompetence or not caring. In general, we frequently find that there are more feelings and damaged relationships to sort out than initially meets the eye.

Although potentially stigmatising, when the diagnosis of ADHD is finally made, things can really start to improve all round. Ideally, everyone already involved has been involved in the assessment and will now be able to assist in putting the management plan into practice. It is essential to attempt to recognise the thoughts, feelings and actions of all concerned. Good communication between the members of the ADHD treatment team can prevent a lot of misunderstandings, and ensure that everyone's efforts are directed in the direction most helpful for the child or young person concerned.

Doctors and other mental health workers involved with a child with ADHD will probably utilise a number of different 'therapies'. They will probably make up a tailor-made package of care to meet the child's own personal needs, in his own personal life situation. Whenever possible, it is important to enlist the help of all able and willing adults.

We will not attempt to describe in detail the theory behind, and exactly how the various psychological therapies are carried out, as to do this would require an entire textbook or two. It will briefly describe the most common psychological interventions for children with ADHD.

Parent Training and Behavioural Therapy

Although most parents are very sensible, most would agree that any practical help and suggestions that might actually work are very welcome.

Years of living with a child with severe ADHD will have taken their toll. Parents may have dug themselves into a hole that is rather hard to get out of, as a result of responding to the behaviours of their child, in a way that seemed reasonable at the time.

Many ADHD children are particularly oppositional. All are at times quite exhausting and irritating company. Whereas it's probably true to say that this applies to most children, children with ADHD are particularly hard work.

Parent training techniques often primarily involve working with parents, and not directly with the child. The therapist will spend time exploring the full extent and nature of the difficulties, how they may have arisen, and how parents have coped so far. They will then work with the parents to develop strategies that are appropriate to their families, based on sound psychological advice, and help them put things into practice.

Often parents will experience a reaction against the new way of doing things. Many parents report that immediately after they have implemented a new behavioural programme, the number and severity of undesired behaviours increases. Things will improve if parents persist with the changes that they have made. The therapist will be needed to support them in doing it. Clearly it is best only to have one set of rules in a family, and parents need to agree to and stick to the same methods, in addition to applying them to all the children, in a similar, but age-appropriate way.

Help with improving parents' abilities to control their children's unwanted behaviour, and to increase the amount of desired behaviour can be provided by various trained professionals. In real life it is often in rather short supply. Some areas have special group programmes for parents, perhaps run by social services or the health visitors. Any plan of action should take into account the child's ADHD symptoms, and the effect they have had on him or her to date. A cookery-book style to parenting is not usually particularly effective in real life.

It is important to remember that even if parents have tried this approach in the past without great success, it may work now. The child is older and he or she may be receiving medication for a condition of which he or she has a greater understanding. Just as some people are more expert at playing tennis than others, some will also have a real knack for applying the principles of behavioural management.

Some parents have found that they gain a great deal of help from some of the excellent books and videos designed for parents. A technique called '1-2-3 Magic' (Phelan 1995) has proved to be of help to a lot of parents of children with ADHD. Many parents are able to find their own way of doing things, and are highly successful, if they are given a few tips and clues.

Many of the techniques used to improve children's behaviour have their theoretical roots in the field of behaviour therapy.

Behavioural therapy is a technique that is increasingly being used to treat a number of mental health problems. Properly adapted it can be successfully used with children with ADHD.

Behavioural therapy involves building up an understanding of how events, thoughts, feelings, and behaviours are linked. The therapist uses real examples from the child's life to do this, and aims to enable them to apply this understanding to difficulties that occur in everyday life.

This therapy is based on the idea that all behaviours are learned, and that therefore they can be unlearned. Unfortunately it is not always as simple as that! There are several behavioural techniques to help to control the unwanted behaviour of children with ADHD specifically. This book cannot describe all those that are successful in detail. To help parents to gain a greater understanding of behavioural methods books and videos that describe them in detail are listed in Appendix III to this book.

Two main behavioural approaches have been shown to be of particular use in reducing unwanted behaviour of children with ADHD. These are called ABC Analysis and the Positive Reinforcement.

ABC Analysis

This is based in the notion that the expression of most behaviour is influenced by *Antecedent* events (what happened before the *Behaviour*) and *Consequent* response (what happened following the behaviour). Altering the antecedents or consequences of any unwanted behaviour may change the frequency of occurrence.

The therapist will ask parents to record the events happening prior to the child's unwanted behaviour. Then the therapist and parents together need to look into any kind of pattern that may illustrate how that the child exhibits the unwanted behaviour in certain circumstances.

The undesired behaviour may occur in specific places (shopping centres, supermarkets, and birthday parties...), at certain times of the day (when he is back from school, following a restless night, before dinner...), and so forth.

A clear description of what the child does and says will help the therapist to understand what the parents and child are experiencing.

Parents will also be asked to record the events happening following the child's behaviour. This encourages them to think about their own responses to the behaviour, and any gains that the child may acquire as a result of his behaviour. Sometimes whilst attempting to stop the unwanted behaviour, parents inadvertently reinforce it and may increase the frequency at which it occurs.

For example, a child who enjoys playing on the computer in his bedroom, rather than sitting quietly and talking with visitors, might behave in such a way that his parents are compelled to 'punish' him by sending him to his room. By responding in this way his parents, who have responded to the undesired behaviour from their child by sending him to his bedroom for 'time out' may find that the child continues to misbehave in the same way.

In this example the punishment actually represents the reward that the child desires. In responding to the undesired behaviour by sending the child to their room, the parents have inadvertently reinforced the behaviour. It is very likely that the next time visitors come, and the child wishes to go to his room to play computer games, that he will behave badly again.

The therapist, together with the parents, will want to change some of the events that take place before and after the unwanted behaviour. These changes may produce a considerable reduction in the child's unwanted behaviour. During the first sessions parents need to work very closely with the therapists until they became familiar with the concepts and the aims of the therapy. A brief summary of this technique is described in the following table.

ABC ANALYSIS

Antecedent events, such as:

1. What was happening before the unwanted behaviour?

2. Who was present when the unwanted behaviour occurred?

3. Where did the behaviour occur?

4. What time of the day did the behaviour occur?

*Description of the **Behaviour**:*

1. How is the onset of the behaviour?

2. What did the child do or say?

3. How frequently does this behaviour happen?

4. How severe is this behaviour?

5. How long does this unwanted behaviour last for?

Consequences, such as:

1. Changes in the demands and expectations of the child by others following the unwanted behaviour

2. Changes in the amount of attention that the child receives following the unwanted behaviour

3. Attainment of child's immediate goals and wants

Positive Reinforcement

Responses to stimuli, or behaviour of any kind, become more frequent or stronger if they lead to rewarding consequences. This concept is utilised by behavioural therapists in a technique called 'positive reinforcement". Parents need to:

° *Specify* with the child the behaviour that they expect from him or her, as precisely as possible. They should try to ensure that the child understands what kind of behaviour is acceptable and what is not. Parents should try to explain what they mean by certain terms such as 'being good', or 'being naughty'. Some of those terms can be confusing for a child, for example 'I like the way you share your sweets with your sister', 'I like the way you tidy your toys before your grandma arrives', 'I don't like the way you shout and scream in the queue of the supermarket'. Parents will need to comment clearly on a child's behaviour; this way the child can start to understand what is expected from them.

° *Explain* to the child the consequences of any good behaviour, so the child is aware of when and what he or she is going to get if he or she behaves appropriately.

° *Reward* the child for the desired behaviour in order to make the child believe that he can succeed. It is important to start to praise or to reward the good behaviour.

° *Ignore* (within reason) undesired behaviour. If children are always in trouble for something, they become discouraged and they may even give up trying to be good. By changing what a child hears about him- or herself from 'bad' to 'good', he or she may become encouraged to act in a way that generates more praise.

° *Help* the child to attain the desired behaviour by planning ahead. Parents should try not to put the child in situations where he or she is more likely to fail, for example taking the child to the supermarket when it is really busy, queues are long and tempers are short.

Every child is different. Some rewards will work for some children but not for others. There is not much point in using a chocolate ice cream as a reward for a child who doesn't like chocolate or ice cream. Parents need to find rewards that their child will respond to.

Successful rewards may include going for a walk with mum or dad, playing a game with their grandparents, and so on. Rewards do not have to be expensive. There are cheaper and better alternatives to money and presents. Young children often respond well to star charts or simple praise.

Rewards need to be given as soon as possible after the behaviour has occurred. It is of little use to ask a child with ADHD to wait until the end of the week to get their reward. Rewards should be implemented immediately following the wanted behaviour. Remember that these children by definition lack on patience and are impulsive, so that waiting for a reward will be very difficult and the chances of success will be minimal. It is important not to set the child up to fail.

Specific rewards may lose their appeal after a while, so it is useful to alter rewards every few days as appropriate. With older children self-rewarding can be a useful technique. The therapist or the parents can teach them to monitor and praise themselves for good behaviour.

In order to obtain the biggest chances of success parents should work closely with the therapist. Teachers could also apply some of those principles in schools and parents can learn to think in this way themselves. This technique has been demonstrated to be very effective for children with ADHD.

Other methods commonly used to reduce children's undesired behaviours include 'time-out' and punishment. The latter should only be used with caution, as repeated or unnecessarily harsh punishments can be damaging, and are nearly always counter-productive.

○ *Punishment:* Parents often resort to physical punishment as it may temporarily reduce unwanted behaviour, although such behaviours often re-emerge later, having not been truly extinguished. Prolonged, severe and painful punishment, particularly in an atmosphere of cold, hostile rejection, is very damaging for children. For these resasons punishment is very seldom used as part of a therapeutic programme.

○ *Time out:* This involves taking the child away from the context in which the behaviour occurred, and making them spend an agreed amount of time in an uninteresting, but safe place. The time spent 'out' must be fairly measured, and if the child persists in continuing the behaviour that was the trigger for time out, the 'clock' has to be started again. The time a child spends in time out should not be excessive, and should be appropriate to the child's age and the nature of the misdemeanour.

In the 1950s and 1960s behavioural therapy often had a somewhat mechanical and simplistic approach. Modern approaches advocate a more flexible approach, whilst maintaining that children need and appreciate clear boundaries.

Parents and the therapist need to take the child's age and ability to understand and control their actions, and also the nature of their relationships into consideration. The opportunity to do something practical themselves to alleviate the difficulties that they are encountering appeals to many parents and children.

As reductions in the number of problems, and the amount of quality time together increases, relationships between parents and their child improve.

A combination of medication and behavioural therapy has been shown to be one of the most successful treatments for ADHD.

Even when behavioural techniques alone were not previously successful for the child and their family, there is a strong chance that they will be, once combined with effective treatment medication.

Family Therapy

There are various schools of thought in family therapy, and a variety of professionals have been trained to work in this way. Family therapists will usually regard ADHD as a family problem, not as one that belongs to the diagnosed child. They usually avoid blame, and concentrate on improving communication and understanding between family members in an attempt to help them find their own solutions to the difficulties the ADHD and other important issues have caused.

This method of working is particularly useful to families who are experiencing difficulties in talking without arguments, and in those where relationships between family members are strained, or breaking down.

Individual Work (Psychodynamic Therapy)

Some of the signs and symptoms of ADHD are at least in part the result of earlier life experiences. Those therapists work with children in an individual way. This involves the child being offered individual sessions, at regular intervals, with an experienced, specially trained therapist. This is an opportunity to allow the child to explore his or her thoughts, feelings, relationships and experiences in privacy, without the risk of upsetting their parents, who may be supported by another team member.

The therapist may use play or art or drama, in the form of role-play, to assist young children, or those who find putting feelings into words difficult.

The therapist aims to establish a good, rewarding and beneficial relationship with the child to give him or her a 'good experience', and utilise this relationship to help the child in other areas of life.

For many children this is an excellent way to help make sense of what has happened, and is happening now, and to gain a greater understanding of how they came to be themselves. It can assist them greatly in day-to-day living, and contribute to 'symptom relief', as they gain an understanding of their own behaviour and that of other people.

It is important to remember that bad therapy is worse than no therapy. A good therapist 'should do no harm' although things may prove difficult along the way. A bad therapist may inadvertently cause a lot of problems, which could prove exceptionally difficult to put right. This is not 'a game for amateurs'. Once a child is in therapy, they should be allowed to stay until a suitable point to stop is reached. Some parents feel tempted to withdraw their child if there are not very noticeable changes within a short space of time. The sort of issues that require this sort of therapy are those that take time and commitment to sort out. It is not fair 'to open a can of worms', and then expect the child to be able to 'put the lid back on' themselves.

This sort of approach can be used alone, or in combination with other treatments depending on the individual child's needs.

Psychodynamic therapy is usually available via child mental health teams.

Working with children, particularly children with neuro-biological disorders, requires specialist knowledge, skills, and insight. These skills are essential if the therapist is to be able to gain a clear understanding of the child, the nature of their difficulties, and be able to work with them in a manner that suits their stage of development and temperament. Only appropriately skilled, trained, and supervised therapists should undertake this sort of work.

Problem Solving Skills

Many of the young people we work with have a lot of difficulty in working out how to solve problems. Helping them involves looking at the problems a child experiences, and helping them to look at possible courses of action, the likely impact of these courses of action, choosing which one to take, and reviewing success or otherwise. This may sound rather obvious, but in reality this is a way of thinking and behaving that is incredibly difficult to learn if you are burdened with the typical 'ADHD' way of thinking.

Conclusion

Finally, one of the most crucial aspects of managing ADHD, regardless of the management plan, is to maintain the spirit of optimism at all times. Most of the families and children have faced repeated failure, rejection and frustration for longer than they care to remember. Many have considered giving up, others already have. 'Help starts now!' should be the theme from the moment assessment begins.

With determination, skilled help and a little luck, things should start to improve from the moment it is realised that something is seriously amiss.

Most young people will be relieved to discover that there are ways of helping that actually work, and will want to be involved in decision making from the beginning. Educating the child and family in a sensitive and constructive way will enable them to participate fully and empower them to be able eventually to solve successfully many ADHD-related difficulties independently. with success. The child or young person should be actively involved in identifying priorities for action, and determining goals and deadlines for them to be achieved, and will need the support of their family and professional helpers every step of the way.

It will probably take a long time and quite a lot of mistakes to reach the goals that have been set, but if these have been broken down into manageable steps, and the time-scale is realistic, success, acceptance, and satisfaction will increase daily.

There are numerous other psychological ways of dealing with the problems encountered, such as neurolinguistic programming, and bio-feedback. Some of these have been proven to work, others have not. The NHS is not able to offer all these therapies, but appropriate use of the methods outlined above will be effective in the vast majority of cases.

CHAPTER II

Education

Children with ADHD often experience difficulties at school because of their core symptoms of inattention, hyperactivity and impulsivity, and the consequences of the sequelae of these. They may also develop superimposed conditions such as depression and behavioural disorders such as conduct disorder and oppositional defiant disorder. These will also affect the child's behaviour and ability to learn in school.

Children with ADHD exhibit the following learning problems:

° 90 per cent are under-productive in schoolwork

° 90 per cent underachieve in school

° 20 per cent have reading difficulties

° 60 per cent have serious handwriting difficulties

° 30 per cent drop out of school in the USA

° 5 per cent of them complete a four-year degree course in a college or university in the USA, compared with approximately 25 per cent of the general population.

Some of these problems, associated with ADHD, are the product of poor motivation and low self-esteem, which may be the result of the inappropriate way that children with ADHD are treated by parents and teachers. Although children with learning difficulties have an increased chance of having ADHD symptoms, many of those with ADHD are intelligent children who are in effect handicapped by the core symptoms. As such they generally underperform and underachieve in school, although people who know them well will realise that their results rarely reflect their innate intelligence.

They are often further hampered by the specific learning difficulties they have with reading and writing. As our educational system relies so heavily on good literacy skills, both to learn and to succeed in assessments and examinations, a lot of these children do not really benefit as much as they should from their time in school.

Because resources are also short in the education system, only the children who really are failing badly usually receive extra help. Many of the children we treat are not only failing and destined for a career below that which they ought to achieve, but have frequently been sent home or have been excluded. Recent research shows that 40 per cent of primary school children excluded from mainstream education had clinical levels of hyperactivity that suggest that these children suffer from ADHD (Arcelus and Munden 1999). Many of them are on the brink of being permanently excluded. Although they have almost certainly been recognised as 'problems', the underlying cause of their difficulties has been missed, and they have not received the help that would have prevented the crises in the first place.

In part this is due to lack of awareness and appropriate training. Many teachers see the problems, can describe them, but do not always realise that they represent a treatable condition.

Other reasons that could explain why ADHD is not always recognised in school are related to the different theoretical perspective taken by different professional groups. Some educational psychologists (and the education system in general) tend to think of children with difficulties in terms of having educational and behavioural difficulties. This is an umbrella term that is used to describe children who display patterns of behaviour and/or emotional expression that have negative effects on their own learning, and/or the learning environment of other children.

Over recent decades there has been an increasing reluctance to medicalise individuals, and label them in a way that emphasises their disabilities, rather than their positive potential. This shift has led to a tendency not to think about 'what is wrong' and 'why?' but to 'what are their needs and how can we help?' The emphasis in special needs education is now on 'learning difficulties' *per se* as opposed to different categories of disability or handicap.

The obvious downside of this is that children with recognisable neurobiological disorders may receive appropriate educational help, but are not referred on to receive the appropriate medical, psychological and social help that will make all the difference.

There are several excellent books and videos that describe how teachers can best assist children with ADHD, which should be available to your child's teacher through the Special Educational Needs Department.

Many of the classroom interventions that have been shown to assist these children in learning, actually benefit most other children, and may already be in place in a well managed classroom setting.

Things that may help include:

° Sitting the child concerned close to the teacher, so that a discrete encouraging eye can be kept on them, breaking big tasks into smaller ones.

° Rewarding good work and sustained attention with praise.

° Light relief in the form of running errands 'to help' when energy and enthusiasm start to flag.

Teachers can be of enormous help in several ways, by:

° Recognising that there is a real problem, not of the child's making, that is treatable.

° Being able to give the child a 'fresh start', once the cause of their difficulties has been identified.

° Encouraging, supporting, and assisting the child: a helpful positive caring adult can be an enormous source of strength for these children, whose experience of school and teachers prior to diagnosis and treatment has usually been less than ideal.

° Finding out about techniques that will help the child to concentrate and to learn, and implementing these techniques.

° Working with the child and their parents, to enable them to tackle areas of difficulty, such as reading, and to catch up/keep up with their peers.

° Assisting medical staff in deciding upon effective medication doses and spacing of doses.

° Encouraging the child to participate in activities that will help to develop self-confidence and social skills.

° Assisting the child in making appropriate choices when choosing a career and examination options.

° Drawing difficulties to the attention of parents and other professionals promptly, so action can be taken before things get out of control.

° Whenever possible trying to find alternatives to exclusion from school, because the effects of that can be irreversibly devastating. Is there a treatable cause for the offending behaviour?

There are a number of books and videos written specifically for teachers and educationalists, and acquiring one (or more) of these should prove to be an invaluable addition to the school's special educational resource needs. See Appendix III for examples.

In practice, teachers attempting to confront numerous demands often feel that they are fighting a losing battle. No matter how well meaning and patient they are it is simply not possible to meet the child's needs without extra help.

Parents may be able to assist the school in gaining extra provision for their child. In the UK there is a Code of Practice on the Identification and Assessment of Special Educational Needs, and either the parent, or the school can request a statutory assessment of their child's needs. The local educational authority will carry this out, and if it identifies sufficient needs, the child will be 'statemented', and a document concerning these needs will be drawn up. The education authority is bound by law to meet these needs.

Of course, a well-designed and integrated inter-agency action plan for ADHD could potentially save a great deal of time, distress and energy for all concerned. A screening programme to identify children with possible ADHD early, with prompt referral for a medical assessment and, if appropriate, effective treatment, combined with appropriate psychological and educational interventions, would certainly prevent many children with ADHD running into serious and very expensive difficulties. It would cost money, require more trained staff than are currently available, and be time consuming, but may even save money in the long run. Such a scheme would probably exist in Utopia, but as yet remains to be implemented here.

In the UK today, all the key agencies involved in the effective recognition and treatment of ADHD (and other mental health difficulties in children), including the NHS, education system, and social services have major difficulties meeting the demands placed upon them. They simply do not have the resources or personnel to cope with the increasing number of referrals that increased recognition of ADHD has led to. In reality, what they can do may well be limited, as they must attempt to treat all children in difficulty.

CHAPTER 12

Social Services and Voluntary Agencies

Once the child's symptoms have been recognised, perhaps even diagnosed, there are a lot of ways that they can be helped, by the family and community at large, and by social services.

Social Services

Social services may be able to help in a number of ways, depending on the child's family's circumstance of the child's family. They can help by:

- Advising informally about the help available that may be appropriate to the child's family. They should be able to advise on how to approach both professional and voluntary agencies, such as the local housing department, the DHSS benefit system, parent training groups, and facilities available for youngsters, including social clubs and holiday activity schemes.

- Assisting in crisis situations on a short-term basis; for example, if a single mother has to be admitted to hospital and needs help in finding somewhere safe and appropriate for her child to stay.

- When appropriate, allocating the child/family a social worker who will become personally involved in resolving difficulties, supporting them through difficult times, offering practical assistance (such as helping them to fill in benefit forms), and enlisting the help of other agencies as appropriate.

° Some social services departments operate schemes (the Befriender schemes) whereby a carefully selected volunteer is introduced to the child to take them out and broaden their horizons whilst developing a supportive relationship. As they have not been involved throughout the child's life they are able to take a fresh perspective, and offer the child a fresh start, unaffected by painful memories and the frustration and weariness that sometimes overwhelms those who have been more closely involved.

° Sometimes there will be quite a lot of different professionals and agencies involved. In the same way that GPs co-ordinate medical care, allocated social workers often take a lead role in co-ordinating multi-agency treatment teams.

Voluntary Sector

When it comes to leading a normal life, voluntary agencies can be of enormous help in enabling families with a child with ADHD to make new friends and establish new interests. Involvement with youth clubs, taking up a new sport or making 'a contribution' through undertaking voluntary work themselves, can really boost young people's self-confidence, social skills, and sense of self-esteem. As young people get older it becomes increasingly important to them to be able to establish friends and interests outside the family home and school. Considering the difficulties many young people with ADHD have experienced in their personal lives before gaining control over their symptoms, opportunities to develop their own friendships and interests are of paramount importance. Many families find that it takes time and effort to find suitable activities, and they often need to persuade the young person and others 'to have a go'. Many people running activities may be wary of accepting a child with ADHD or behavioural problems, but are reassured once they understand exactly what is required of them, and how the child is likely to respond.

Benefits

In the UK some families find that their child qualifies for Disability Living Allowance, and that they qualify for Carer's Allowance, amongst other benefits. Families may find that it is worth talking to the DHSS, the Citizen's Advice Bureau, or their social worker about such entitlements. These benefits can enable children and young people to undertake the sort of activities that will help them to develop as mature, capable members of society, and so often make all the difference to their future. It is also a way of providing parents with a break that allows them to recuperate, and go on caring for their child without becoming worn down, exhausted or socially isolated. At the time of going to press, the benefits available to young people with ADHD and their families within the United Kingdom include:

°   Disability Living Allowance (paid at three levels according to the amount of care and supervision required, worth £13.60, £34.30, and £51.30 per week). The child, if over five years of age and not able to walk, may also be entitled to a 'mobility component' (worth £13.60 or £35.85 per week).

°   Invalid Care Allowance for the main carer (£38.70 per week), if they provide more than 35 hours' care per week, are not in full time education, and have an income of less than £50 per week. This is only payable to the carers of children receiving the middle or higher rates of Disability Living Allowance.

In order to claim Disability Living allowance, it is crucial that the completed forms are worded so as to illustrate clearly how the child's symptoms and abilities meet the qualifying criteria. People who probably know very little about ADHD will process any claim. It is necessary to demonstrate that although the child is able to walk and dress and so forth, they pose a risk to themselves, and need a level of supervision that exceeds that usually required for a child of that age.

Our experience suggests that when a child really is affected to a degree that qualifies them to receive extra benefits, the factor that determines whether they get it or not seems to be the way the questionnaires are completed. Both parents and the professionals who they recommend to the DHSS to report on their behalf must be fully aware of the symptoms and difficulties involved and clearly relate those to the qualifying criteria. The way that benefits are calculated is complicated. If the above benefits are awarded, other benefits that the family is receiving might need to be adjusted. Families on low income, or living on benefits, or in which one parent does not work, might be eligible to apply. The value of the benefits also alters regularly, so families (living in the UK) are advised to contact Benefits Enquiry Line on Freephone 0800 882200 for further advice and to request forms.

CHAPTER 13

Long-Term Prospects for Children with ADHD

It appears that some people will 'grow out' of their ADHD with time, with approximately half of affected children appearing to function normally by young adulthood. The rest will continue to have significant difficulties throughout life.

Overall, 30–80 per cent of diagnosed hyperactive children will continue to have symptoms that persist into adult life. If their ADHD is recognised and adequately treated, it should be possible to find a career and lifestyle in which they flourish without causing major difficulties in their lives.

It seems that a family history of ADHD, the presence of psychosocial adversities, and co-morbidity with conduct, mood and anxiety symptoms increase the risk of persistence of symptoms.

Current research suggests that within the 'diagnostic umbrella' of ADHD (a group of disorders with the same type of symptomatology) there are a number of sub-types. In particular, researchers have suggested that those with ADHD and anxiety-type symptoms have a different outcome, and respond differently to treatment from those with more prominent aggressive and anti-social traits. Early onset conduct disorder, occurring in the presence of ADHD, has been noted to be associated with a high incidence of criminality, aggression and drug and alcohol abuse later in life. Research is currently under way to clarify which types of treatment (e.g. medication, parent training, cognitive behavioural therapy) are most effective for different types of patients, and at what stage they are best implemented.

In the meantime, it seems most prudent to attempt to identify children with ADHD and to implement effective treatment and intervention strategies as early as possible. This presents a considerable challenge to those professionals involved in the health, education and social services. It is imperative that they continue to work in collaboration with the family support groups so active in the United Kingdom, to ensure that this potentially treatable group of young people and adults do not suffer needlessly.

Many of the symptoms and characteristics of ADHD can be turned to the child's advantage. Some ideas and true accounts of other people's experiences can be found in Thom Hartmann's book, *ADHD Success Stories* (see Appendix III at the end of this book).

The future for people with ADHD need not be bleak. By taking stock of the child's strengths and weaknesses, and ensuring that they receive appropriate help, families and professionals can work together to ensure that the young person realises their full potential, and goes on to lead a happy and successful life.

CHAPTER 14

ADHD in Adults

There is an increasing awareness of the continuation of symptoms of ADHD extending from childhood, through adolescence and into adult life in some young people. The recognition and provision of assessment and treatment for adults in the UK is lagging behind the treatment facilities for children and adolescents. Fortunately there is a fast-growing recognition of the disorder amongst adult psychiatrists. Adult mental health services will need to set up treatment facilities for young adults, who started to receive treatment in their childhood by child and adolescent psychiatrists.

There are rapidly rising numbers of referrals being made to child and adolescent mental health services for ADHD. This is resulting in ever-increasing numbers of young people requiring regular monitoring of medication and on-going psychotherapeutic help for ADHD accumulating on consultants' case lists, who will not be able to provide on-going treatment for these young people as they enter adult life.

Epidemiology: How Frequently Do Adults Suffer from ADHD?

Studies following children diagnosed with ADHD over time have demonstrated that the symptoms will persist in a significant number of them into adult life. Studies described by Denckla *et al.* (1976), have demonstrated that between 31 per cent and 66 per cent of adults with a history of childhood ADHD continue to have symptoms of the disorder. This will mean that around 1–2 per cent of adults will fulfil the diagnostic criteria for ADHD.

Making a Diagnosis: Diagnostic Criteria

Neither DSM-IV nor ICD-10, the diagnostic classification systems currently in use in the field of mental health make any stipulation about the age at which the diagnosis can be made. They are concerned that symptoms should have been present from early childhood, and should be present to a degree that is abnormal for a person of that age and mental capacity, or intelligence, and to cause significant functional impairment. Until recently, it was generally assumed that ADHD occurred predominantly in childhood, and gradually burnt itself out through adolescence. Consequently many of the diagnostic criteria for ADHD in children are not directly applicable to adults (e.g. 'has difficulty playing quietly', difficulty awaiting his/her turn in games').

As it has become apparent that the core symptoms of in-attention, hyperactivity and impulsivity persist into adult life in some cases, and continue to cause disability, attempts have been made to design a different set of diagnostic criteria for use with adults.

The Utah Criteria

The so-called 'Utah' Criteria were developed by Paul Wender and his colleagues for use in research projects regarding the efficacy of pharmacological treatments in adults with ADHD (Wender *et al.* 1971). To fulfil these criteria a history of symptoms of ADHD in childhood must be established and the two following character-istics should be present in adulthood:

1. *Persistent motor hyperactivity* such as the inability to relax, inability to persist in sedentary activities such as reading, or watching television, and dysphoria when inactive.

2. *Attention deficits* manifested by the inability to keep one's mind on a conversation, reading materials, or his or her job. Distractibility and forgetfulness demonstrated by actions such as losing or misplacing items.

In addition to this at least two of the following characteristics must be present:

1. *Affective lability* with mood swings lasting hours to a few days, that range from being bored and discontented to being excited.

2. *Inability to complete tasks* which includes: A lack of organisation at work or at home, the inability to solve problems and manage time, and the inability to concentrate on one task at a time.

3. *Temper problems* such as: being irritable, easily provoked, and explosive.

4. *Impulsivity* such as: non-reflective decision making, which also results in turbulent work performance and personal relationships, antisocial behaviours and reckless pleasure-seeking activities.

5. *Low tolerance for stress* which results in: depression, anxiety, confusion, or anger from just having to deal with typical everyday situations.

The diagnosis is precluded by diagnoses of schizophrenia, schizo-affective disorder, primary affective disorder, and schizotypal or borderline personality disorder. (That is, such a diagnosis can't be made if any of these conditions are present.)

Other Mental Illnesses that Can Occur with ADHD in Adults

Adults who meet the Utah criteria for ADHD have a high incidence of concurrent psychopathology. Like many children with ADHD they may also have another, more time-limited illness or disorder.

Shekim and his colleagues (1985) demonstrated that of 56 adults aged 19–65 years, who met the Utah criteria for adult ADHD:

- ° 53 per cent also met diagnostic criteria for generalised anxiety disorder

- ° 34 per cent also met diagnostic criteria for alcohol abuse or dependence

- ° 30 per cent also met diagnostic criteria for drug abuse

- ° 25 per cent also met diagnostic criteria for dysthymia (chronic low mood which is disabling, but not severe enough to fulfil diagnostic criteria for depressive disorders)

- ° 25 per cent also met diagnostic criteria for cyclothymic disorder (in which the sufferer has disabling mood swings that alternate from 'high' to 'low', but not with such intensity as would be required to meet the diagnostic criteria for Manic Depressive Disorders).

Only 14 per cent met the diagnostic criteria for ADHD alone, and one third had four additional diagnoses in addition to ADHD. ADHD appears to be a frequent underlying factor in the development of pathological gambling.

The Effect of ADHD on the Sufferer's Life

As in childhood and adolescence, the underlying triad of core ADHD symptoms can make the lives for sufferers and those around them difficult.

Attention Deficit can lead to difficulties following lectures and meetings, and also during in-depth reading. Adults may be easily side-tracked, missing information, overlooking details and making careless mistakes. They make errors in spelling, and in arithmetic, and may take the wrong exit of motorways whilst driving, as they became distracted from the task in hand. This, over the course of their education and throughout their working lives, may have caused them to fail to achieve their full potential, and consequently 'under-achieve'.

Embarrassment can result in social situations as the ADHD sufferer loses track of conversations, and can led to friction in relationships. The difficulties encountered in task planning and personal organisation (often greatly hindered by distractibility) can lead to their being labelled as procrastinators, or lazy and lacking in self-discipline. Countless difficulties can ensue from leaving possessions such as wallets and passports behind, or being late for, or forgetting to attend meetings.

Hyperactivity may or may not be present in adults with ADHD. Some find it impossible to be still, or relatively passive or inactive for any length of time. They may squirm and fidget, altering their position endlessly, in lectures, concerts and the theatre.

Impulsivity can lead to difficulty waiting, for example in restaurants or traffic jams. Adults with ADHD may take un-necessary and irresponsible risks when driving, making reckless attempts to advance their position.

Although not part of the diagnostic criteria for adult ADHD, many clinicians experienced in diagnosing and treating this disorder report excessive mood swings, irritability, and low tolerance to frustration amongst their patients. They often react badly to stress and can become easily depressed.

Assessment and Diagnosis of Adult ADHD

Assessment and diagnosis of adults presenting with possible ADHD should follow broadly similar lines to that undertaken in children. It is likely, however, to be difficult to obtain accurate, relevant retrospective details regarding the person's childhood, necessary to establish that this is indeed a life-long disorder.

The diagnosis remains a clinical one, and needs to be made only after a careful and comprehensive assessment has been carried out. Because of the difficulty in delineating between ADHD and other psychiatric diagnoses, and the high incidence of other mental illnesses occurring in adult ADHD sufferers, only psychiatrists who are familiar with ADHD in addition to the other mental health difficulties that occur in adults should make the diagnosis.

The assessment should include a detailed interview with the person in question, and wherever possible, responsible relatives or friends who have known them throughout their lives. Issues to be covered include the presence or absence of the core symptoms of ADHD from childhood, the degree of incapacity and inconvenience they have caused, and attempts to date that have been made to overcome them.

The doctor will need to look for signs and symptoms of other mental illnesses, psychological or behavioural difficulties and personality traits, that could account for the apparent symptoms of ADHD, or occur at the same time. This needs to be set in context against the patient's medical, family, relationship and life histories. The doctor will need to compare this information to that available from other sources, such as relatives, school reports, or correspondence with other professionals who have assessed or worked therapeutically with the patient throughout their life.

The doctor will supplement the information gleaned with a physical examination and other investigations, as outlined earlier in this book. They will need to use behavioural checklists, and might consider using continuous performance tests. Checklists currently in use for the assessment of ADHD in adults include the Wender Utah Rating Scale, the Brown Attention-Activation Disorder Scale (BAADS), the Copeland Symptom Checklist for Adult Attention Deficit Disorder, and Triolo's Attention-Deficit Scales for Adults (ADSA).

Although these checklists lack normative data, and are usually not taken to be diagnostic, they are helpful in establishing the type and degree of symptoms present. Doctors still believe that the

DSM-IV criteria, albeit slightly inappropriate, to be the most recognised, accepted and scientifically verified set of criteria.

The doctor might supplement their assessment by requesting a standardised intelligence test, or using other screening symptom/behaviour checklists, such as depression and anxiety scales, or marital satisfaction scales.

Treatment of Adult ADHD

Medication

Medication remains the first line treatment for adults with ADHD. The drugs listed below have been discussed in detail in the chapter on medication in children with ADHD. The most commonly used classes of drugs include:

1. *Stimulants:* Methylphenidate (Ritalin) is usually the treatment of choice. Other stimulants that have been used include Dexamphetamine (Dexadrine). Unlike in children, of whom approximately 70 per cent with ADHD respond to stimulants, research suggests that between 25–78 per cent of adults (mean 52%) respond to stimulant medication. Adults, like younger patients, may require robust doses of medication to relieve their symptoms effectively, and it is important to increase their medication in step-wise increments to a maximum tolerated dose (monitoring for side effects) before deciding if the stimulants have worked or not.

2. *Tricyclic Antidepressants:* Imipramine and Desipramine are generally considered to be second-line drugs, although many questions regarding their usage still need to be answered. For example, the results of drug trials to date conflict, with some studies suggesting lower doses, whilst others recommend higher doses.

3. *Buspirone:* Another antidepressant shown to be effective. This is an atypical stimulant antidepressant, that appears to have a rapid and sustained effect on the symptoms of

ADHD, and is relatively safe for patients with cardiac abnormalities compared to the older Tricyclic Antidepressants.

4. *Propranolol:* It has been useful in reducing the frequency of temper outbursts and the symptoms of ADHD.

5. *Anxiolytic drugs:* These are taken to reduce levels of anxiety in the patient. They have also been proposed as helpful drugs for the treatment of adult ADHD.

6. *Other medication:* Fluoxetine (Prozac, an SSRI antidepressant), Clonidine (an antihypertensive drug), Thioridazine (an antipsychotic drug), Carbamazepine (a mood stabiliser) and Lithium Carbonate (a mood stabiliser) have been shown to be effective in some adults with ADHD.

All there medications need further evaluation, in order to establish which drugs, and in which dose range, should be used in adults with ADHD.

Non-Pharmacological Treatments for Adults with ADHD

There will be many issues for adults with ADHD that need to be resolved that do not respond to medication. These may include low self-esteem, emotional and social isolation, feelings of rage, time-management difficulties, a tendency to procrastinate, and avoidance of difficult tasks.

The adult with ADHD will need to discuss these with the psychiatrist who is responsible for their care, and a management plan that takes on board their psychological/psychotherapeutic needs, in addition to social and employment issues should be drawn up. Many of the techniques described earlier in this book are applicable to adults, and the psychiatrist may be able to involve other members of the adult mental health team in assisting their patient.

Much remains to be done in the field of ADHD as it occurs in adults, particularly regarding clinical research to resolve the numerous questions that need to be answered. In the UK there is a need to develop effective and appropriate assessment and treatment services rapidly.

We retain the hope that if awareness of ADHD and effective interventions continues to increase and people with ADHD are recognised and treated early in life, many of the difficulties can be prevented.

Some Useful Assessment Instruments

Instrument	Checklist/ Continuous Performance Test	Information Yielded	Source
Du Paul Questionnaire	ADHD symptom checklist	Presence and severity of symptoms felt to be present by person completing form, with some indication of symptom severity	See reference Du Paul (1991)
DSM-IV Symptom Checklist	ADHD symptom checklist	As above	See reference Gordon (1995)
Home and School Situation Questionnaires	Checklists to demonstrate severity of symptoms of ADHD in different environments	As above	As above, and reference Barkley and Edelbrock (1987)
Child Behaviour Checklist, Youth Self Report, and Teachers Report Form (Achenbach)	Checklists that screen for a wide variety of symptoms that occur in young people, including symptoms of withdrawal, somatisation, social function, attention, delinquency and aggression	An impression of the nature, breadth and severity of the difficulties experienced by the young person compared to others of the same age and sex. Computerised analysis and cross-referencing allows comparison of different informants responses.	Enquiries and orders: University Medical Education Associates, One South Prospect St, Rm 6434, Burlington, VT 05401-3456 (UK: Checklist and Allied Services, P.O. Box 3691, Hall Green, Birmingham, B28 0AP. Tel 0121 778 4247) See reference Achenbach and Edelbrock (1981, 1983).

Strengths and Difficulties Questionnaire	An easily and quickly applied checklist of use by parents and teachers, useful for screening for a wide range of difficulties	A brief mental health screening questionnaire, giving balanced coverage of behaviours, emotions and relationships	See reference Goodman (1997)
Gordon Diagnostic System	Continuous Performance Test	Objective measurements of impulse control, vigilance, and dis-tractibility, compared to other children of that age	Enquiries and orders: Gordon Systems, Inc., P.O. Box 746 DeWitt, NY 13214 Tel 315-446-4849 Fx 315-446-2012 See references Gordon (1986, 1987)

Useful Contacts

United Kingdom
ADD Information Services

ADD Information Services is a charitable body that has links with over 150 support groups over the UK – a full list is available on request. They are able to offer advice to parents, young people, and professionals. They can also organise and co-ordinate seminars and conferences for parent support groups and professional organisations. Once a year, in the autumn, ADD Information Services holds an International Conference for parents and professionals, inviting eminent professionals from all over the world to present lectures and workshops to different groups of delegates, and providing a unique forum for the exchange of ideas in an informal setting.

ADD Information Services also stock most of the books and videos listed below, and can supply these promptly by mail order. For further information send a large SAE or contact: Mrs Andrea Bilbow, PO Box 340, Edgware, Middlesex HA8 9HL. Tel: 0181 905 2013. Fax: 0181 386 6466. Email: iss@compuserve.com.

The ADHD Family Support Group

This organisation is able to offer accessible advice to parents and professionals, and publishes a regular newsletter mailed to members. For further information send a large SAE to: Mrs Gill Mead, 1A, The High Street, Dilton Marsh, Wiltshire. BA13 4DL. Tel 01373 826045.

ADHD North West

ADHD North West co-ordinate, parent support groups operating in the North West of the UK. This organisation is able to put parents in touch with local 'contact parents' and support groups in their area who are able to offer practical advice and support. For information call Mrs

Barbara Worrall on 01524 822887. Email: worral@addnorthwest. u-net.com.

The Benefits Enquiry Line

This Free-phone number puts parents directly in contact with advisers that are able to discuss and clarify the financial benefits that callers might be able to apply for. They can also send parents the appropriate claim forms. Tel 0800 882200.

The Department for Education and Employment (DfEE)

Elizabeth House, York Road, London SE1 7PH (Code of Practice SEN) Tel 0171 510 0150.

The Advisory Centre for Education

ACE are able to offer parents free personal telephone advice on issues related to education, special educational needs and many other educational issues. They are able to advise parents on how to go about resolving their child's difficulties, by explaining who to approach and what should be said or done. They produce a publication list, which will be of interest to many parents of children with ADHD. For further information contact: (ACE) Ltd, 1B Aberdeen Studios, 22–24, Highbury Grove, London N5 2DQ. Tel 0171 354 8321.

Contact a Family

This organisation is a charity that can put parents of children with ADHD and other medical and psychiatric problems in touch with other parents of young people with similar problems. They can also advise parents of a wide variety of organisations that may be able to offer them help. 170 Tottenham Court Road, London W1P 0HA. Tel 0171 383 3555.

Child Line

24-hour free help line for children. Freephone 0800 1111.

The Samaritans

24-hour service from trained volunteers who will listen and offer advice. Tel 0345 909090.

The Children's Legal Centre
Tel 01206 873820, Mon–Fri, 2–5pm.

IPSEA
Legal advice for special educational needs. Tel 01394 382814.

Kidscape
A registered charity, set up to prevent child abuse and bullying. They are able to work with parents, young people and professionals, and they also organise conferences and workshops. For further information contact: Kidscape at 152, Buckingham Palace Road, London SW1W 9 TR.

Eire
HADD
Stephanie Mahoney, Dublin. Tel 00 3531 288 9766.
Maeve Dale, Dublin. Tel 00 3531 822 2059.

Australia
ADDISS
ADD information and support services. PO Box 1661, Milton, Queensland 4064. Tel 07 33 68 3977.

Learning Disabilites Coalition Group
Sydney, NSW. Tel 02 9542 3390.

United States of America
Support Organisations

C.H.A.D.D. (Children and Adults with Attention Deficit Disorder)
National Headquarters
Suite 308
499 NW 70th Avenue
Plantation, FL 33317
Tel 305-487-3700.

Learning Disabilities Association (LDA)
4156 Library Road

Pittsburgh, PA 15234
Tel 412-341-1515.

Legal Resources

Department of Justice
Office of Americans with Disabilities Act
Civil Rights Division
PO Box 66118
Washington, DC 20035
Tel 202-514-0301.

Office of Special Education and Rehabilitative Services
330 C Street SW
Switzer Building Room 3006
Washington, DC 20202-2500
Tel 202-205-5507.

Call this office for help with Section 504 of the Rehabilitation Act or with the Individuals with Disabilities Education Act (IDEA).

ADHD on the Internet

www.web-tv.co.uk/addnet.html
The ADD net home page.

www.chadd.org
US website.

www.pavilion.co.uk/add/english.html
European home page.

www.azstarnet.com/~ash
for adults with ADHD.

www.shef.ac.uk/~psyc/interpsyc'inter.html
A vmental health resource.

www.mediconsult.com/frames/add
A medical information website.

www.accap.org

The home page of the American Academy of Child and Adolescent Psychiatry (fact sheets, research and conference information).

www.addiss.co.uk

The home page of ADD Information Services.

Books and Videos

For Parents

Barkley, R. (1995) *Taking Charge of ADHD, The Complete Authoritative Guide for Parents*
New York: The Guilford Press. ISBN 0-89862-099-6

A comprehensive book written by one of the leading American Authorities for parents, covering a wide range of issues, including information about assessment and diagnosis, research, practical interventions and advice, and advice concerning medication. This book would also be an appropriate source of information for professionals working in the health, education and social services.

Gordon, M. (1991) *ADHD/Hyperactivity: A Consumer's Guide*
New York: DeWitt, GSI

A humourous, easy-to-read book. Professor Gordon answers many of the questions that parents frequently ask about ADHD.

Hartmann, T. *ADHD Success Stories*
Grass Valley, CA: Underwood. ISBN 1887-424-032

An inspiring book, that eloquently recounts the experiences of families and young people, who have turned their lives into success stories.

Phelan, T. (1995) *1-2-3-Magic*
Glen Ellyn, IL: Child Management Inc. ISBN 0-9633861-9-0

A very useful, practical book, that many parents of children with ADHD have found extremely helpful when attempting to cope with their child's behavioural problems.

Rief, S. (1997). *The ADD/ADHD Checklist: An Easy Reference for Parents and Teachers*

Paramus, NJ: Prentice Hall. ISBN 0-13-762395

Highly recommended for parents who are trying to address the difficulties associated with ADHD.

Parker, H. (1988). *The ADD Hyperactivity Workbook for Parents, Teachers and Kids*

Plantation, FL: Speciality Press

A practical, easy-to-use work book, that clearly illustrates how parents and young people can work together, to cope with many of the difficulties that families have to contend with on a daily basis.

For Young People

Nadeau, K. and Dixon, E. (1997) *Learning to Slow Down and Pay Attention*

Washington, DC: Magination Press. ISBN 1-55798-456-5

An overview of ADHD, that focuses on the feelings and emotions of children with ADHD. The book aims to help them gain control of situations, and offers specific techniques to help the child become more organised, function better at school, and to cope with friends. This book is aimed at children aged 8-12 years, and should prove to be of great use to them.

Quinn, P. and Stern, J. (1991) *Putting on the Brakes, Activity Book for Young People.*

Washington, DC: Magination Press. ISBN 0-945 354-32-0

This book allows children to put ideas into practice when trying to overcome their difficulties. It utilises pictures, puzzles, mazes and much more to address tasks such as problem solving, organisation, setting priorities and planning and maintaining control. Aimed at 8-12 year olds.

Gordon, M. *'Jumping' Johnny Get Back to Work!'* and *'My Brother's a World Class Pain'.*

Humourous, well-illustrated books, aimed at younger children, which are very helpful in helping them to understand the pitfalls of ADHD.

Professor Gordon presents an optimistic, but realistic view of how difficulties may be resolved.

Gordon, M. *I Would if I Could: A Teenager's Guide to ADHD.*
A helpful book, aimed at teenagers that answers many questions commonly asked, and explains clearly how difficulties may be approached.

For Adults with ADHD

Wender, P. (1995). *Attention Deficit Hyperactivity Disorder in Adults.*
Oxford University Press. ISBN 0-19-511922-3

A popular guide for adults with ADHD.

Ramundo, P. and Kelly, K. (1996) *You Mean I'm not Lazy, Stupid or Crazy: A Self-Help Book for Adults with Attention Deficit Disorder.*

An excellent book, written by ADD adults for ADD adults, which give practical help and moral support.

For Teachers

Cooper, P. and Ideus, K. (1996) *Attention Deficit/Hyperactivity Disorder, A Practical Guide for Teachers.*
London: David Fulton Publishers Ltd.

A practically orientated book aimed at teachers and educationalists. The authors carefully present information concerning the symptoms, assessment, diagnosis and treatment of ADHD. They include practical strategies for implementation in the classroom, and a number of checklists to facilitate the monitoring of progress. A useful resource for in-house training programmes, and also of great practical help for teachers trying to implement effective educational interventions in the classroom.

Gordon, M. and Parker, H. *Teaching the Child with ADHD: A Slide Program for In-Service Teacher Training.*

This includes 46 professionally produced slides, a presenter's manual, a viewer's guide, and 10 multiple-choice questions that can be adapted for evaluation of continuing education.

For Doctors and Other Health Workers

Dulcan, M. (1997) 'Practice parameters for the assessment and treatment of children, adolescents and Adults with Attention Deficit/Hyperactivity Disorder.' *Journal of the American Academy of Child and Adolescent Psychiatry, 36,* 10, 85–120.

An extremely useful document, including a clear, concise literature review, covering clinical and theoretical aspects of ADHD. It gives clear, precise recommendations for the assessment and treatment of ADHD, endorsed by the American Academy of Child and Adolescent Psychiatry.

Goldstein, S. and Goldstein, M. (1998) *Managing ADHD in Children: A Guide for Practitioners.* Second edition.
New York: John Wiley.

An important resource for professionals working with children and families with ADHD.

Gordon, M. (1995) *How to Operate an ADHD Clinic or Subspecialty Practice.*
New York: GSI Publications.

A detailed comprehensive manual with excellent advice and useful checklists. A humourous and helpful book.

Rosenberg, D., Holttum, J. and Gershon, S. *Textbook of Pharmacotherapy for Child and Adolescent Psychiatric Disorders.*
New York: Brunner/Mazel.

A comprehensive, accessible textbook of paediatric psychopharmacology, containing both clinical and practical information and advice.

Rutter, M., Taylor, E. and Hersov, L. (1994) *Child and Adolescent Child Psychiatry, Modern Approaches.*
Oxford: Blackwell Scientific Publications

A comprehensive and detailed major reference, containing a wealth of information and references, covering most aspects of child and adolescent psychiatry, including 'Disorders of Attention Deficit and Overactivity'.

Spencer, T., Biederman, J., Wilens, T., Harding, M., O'Donnel, D. and Griffin, S. (1996) 'Pharmacotherapy of Attention-Deficit Hyperactivity

Disorder across the life-cycle.' *Journal of the American Academy of Child and Adolescent Psychiatry, 35*, 4, 407–432.

A detailed and comprehensive literature review, presenting a balanced overview of current knowledge regarding the pharmacological treatment of ADHD in a clear and concise way. Much of the data is collated in a clear and easily accessible tabulated form.

For Teachers and Educationalists

Cooper, P. and Ideus, K. (1996) *Attention Deficit/Hyperactivity Disorder, A Practical Guide for Teachers.*
London: David Fulton publishers Ltd

A practically orientated book aimed at teachers and educationalists. The authors carefully present information concerning the symptoms, assessment, diagnosis and treatment of ADHD. They include practical strategies for implementation in the classroom, and a number of checklists to facilitate the monitoring of progress. A useful resource for in-house training programmes, and also of great practical help for teachers trying to implement effective educational interventions in the classroom.

General

Holowenko, H. (1999) *Attention Deficit/Hyperactivity Disorder: A Multidisciplinary Approach.*
London: Jessica Kingsley Publishers.

The author provides carefully described and detailed practical strategies for parents and professionals to implement whilst trying to help young people with ADHD. This book's multidisciplinary approach stresses the collaborative nature of successful management of ADHD. An invaluable book for those asking: 'What can I do to help?'

Videos
There are a number of excellent videos available from ADD Information Services that cover several aspects of ADHD for parent and teachers. There is also a video that accompanies '1-2-3 Magic'. Readers are advised to contact ADD Information Services for an up-to-date list of videos.

Bibliography

Achenbach, T.M. and Edelbrock, C.S. (1981) Behavioural problems and competencies reported by parents of normal and disturbed children aged four through sixteen. *Monographs for the Society of Research in Child Development 46, 2.*

Achenbach, T.M. and Edelbrock, C.S. (1983) *Manual for the Child Behaviour Checklist and Revised Child Behaviour Profile.* University of Vermont, Burlington, Department of Psychiatry.

American Psychiatric Association (1994). *Diagnostic and Statistical Manual of Mental Disorders* (4th ed.). Washington, DC: American Psychiatric Press.

Arcelus, J. and Munden, A.C. (1999) *Symptoms of ADHD and Emotional and Behavioural Disturbance in Children from Mainstream Education.*

Barkley, R.A. (1995). *Taking Charge of ADHD, The Complete Authoritative Guide for Parents.* New York: Guilford Press.

Barkley, R.A. and Edelbrock, C. (1987) 'Assessing situational variation in children's problem behaviours: The Home and School Situations Questionnaires.' *Advances in Behavioural Assessment of Children and Families 3,* 157–176.

Battle, E.S., and Lacey, B. (1972). 'A context of hyperactivity in children over time.' *Child Development,* 43, 757–773.

Biederman, J., Faraone, S.V., Keenan, K., Knee, D. (1990). 'Family-genetic and psychosocial risk factors in DSM-III attention deficit disorder.' *Journal of the American Academy of Child and Adolescent Psychiatry 29,* 526–533.

Bradley, C. (1937) 'The behaviour of children receiving Benzedrine.' *American Journal of Psychiatry 94,* 826–836.

Brandon, S. (1971) 'Overactivity in childhood.' *Journal of Psychosomatic Research,* 15, 411–415.

Buschbaum, M. and Wender, P. (1973) 'Average evoked responses in normal and minimally brain dysfunctional children treated with Amphetamine.' *Archives of General Psychiatry 29,* 6, 764–770.

Comings, D. (1990) *Tourette Syndrome and Human Behaviour.* Duoste, CA: Hope Press.

Conners, C.K. (1969) 'A teacher rating scale for use in drug studies with children.' *American Journal of Psychiatry 126,* 884–888.

Conners, C.K. (1973) Rating scales for use in drug studies with children.' *Psychopharmacology Bulletin, Special Issue,* 24–84.

Cooper, P. and Ideus, K. (1996). *Attention Deficit/Hyperactivity Disorder, A Practical Guide for Teachers.* London: David Fulton Publishers Ltd.

Denkle, M. Bemparad, J. and Mackay, M. (1976) 'Tics following Methylphenidate administration: A report of twenty cases.' *Journal of the American Medical Association 235,* 1349–1351.

Dulcan, M. (1997) 'Practice parameters for the assessment and treatment of children, adolescents, and adults With attention deficit/hyperactivity disorder.' *Journal of American Academy of Child and Adolescent Psychiatry 36,* 10, 85–120.

Du Paul, G. J. (1991) 'Inter-rater reliability of teacher rating scales for children with Attention-Deficit Hyperactivity Disorders.' *Journal of Psychopathology and Behavioural Assessments 18,* 227–237.

Fiefel, D. (1996). 'Attention-Deficit Hyperactivity Disorder in adults.' *Postgraduate Medicine,* 100, 207–218.

Freeman, R. (1977) 'Psychiatric aspects of sensory disorders and intervention.' In P. Graham (ed) *Epidemiological Approaches in Child Psychiatry.* London: Academic Press.

Freeman, R., Malkin, S. and Hasting, S.J. (1975) 'Psychological problems of deaf children and their families: A comparative study.' *American Annals of the Deaf 120,* 391–405.

Gilger, J.W., Pennington, B.F., and DeFries, J.C. (1992) 'A twin study of the etiology of co-morbidity: Attention Deficit Hyperactivity Disorder and dyslexia.' *Journal of the American Academy of Child and Adolescent Psychiatry,* 31, 343–348.

Gillberg, C., Carlstrom, G. and Rasmussen, P. (1983) 'Hyperkinetic disorders in children with perceptual, motor and attention deficits.' *Journal of Child Psychology and Psychiatry 24,* 233–246.

Goodman, R. (1994) 'Brain disorders.' In M. Rutter, E. Taylor and L. Hersov (eds) *Child and Adolescent Psychiatry, Modern Approaches.* Oxford: Blackwell Science Ltd.

Goodman, R. (1997) 'The Strengths and Difficulties Questionnaire: A research note.' *Journal of Child Psychology and Psychiatry 38,* 5, 581–586.

Gordon, M. (1986) 'Microprocessor-based assessment of Attention Deficit Disorders.' *Psychopharmacology Bulletin 22,* 288–290.

Gordon, M. (1987) 'How is a computerised attention test used in the diagnosis of Attention Deficit Disorder?' In J. Loney (ed) *The Young Hyperactive Child: Answers to Questions about Diagnosis, Prognosis and Treatment.* New York: Haworth Press.

Gordon, M. (1995). *How to Operate an ADHD Clinic or Subspecialty Practice.* New York: GSI Publications.

Hartmann, T. *ADD – A Different Perspective.* Grass Valley, CA: Underwood Books.

Hill, P. (1989) 'Psychiatric aspects of children's head injury.' In D.A. Johnson, D. Ultrey and M. Wyke (eds) *Children's Head Injury: Who Cares?* Philadelphia: Taylor and Francis.

Hoare, P. 'Development of psychiatric disorder among school children with epilepsy.' *Developmental Medicine and Child Neurology 26,* 14–19.

Hoare, P. (1993) *Essential Child Psychiatry.* London: Churchill Livingstone.

Hoare, P. and Kevley, S. (1991) 'Psychological adjustment of children with avaric epilepsy and their families.' *Developmental Medicine and Child Neurology 33,* 201–215.

Hynd, G.W., Semrud-Clikerman, M., Lorys, A.R., Novey, E.S., and Eliopulos, D. (1990) 'Brain morphology in developmental dyslexia and attention deficit/hyperactivity.' *Archives of Neurology,* 47, 919–926.

Hynd, G.W., Semrud-Clikerman, M., Lorys, A.R., Novey, E.S., Eliopulos, D., and Lyytinen, H. (1991) 'Corpus callosum morphology in Attention Deficit/Hyperactivity Disorder; morphometric analysis of MRI.' *Journal of Learning Disabilities,* 24, 141–146.

Jenson, P., Mrazek, D., Knapp, P., Steinberg, L., Pfeffer, C., Schowalter, J. and Shapiro, T. (1997) 'Evolution and revolution in child psychiatry: ADHD as a disorder of adaptation.' *Journal of the American Academy of Child and Adolescent Psychiatry 36,* 12, 1672–1681.

Kuhne, M., Schachar, R, and Tannock, R. (1997) 'Impact of comorbid oppositional or conduct problems on attention-deficit hyperactivity disorder.' *Journal of the American Academy of Child and Adolescent Psychiatry 36,* 12, 1715–1725.

Lesaca T. (1994) 'An overview of adulthood attention deficit hyperactivity disorder.' *The West Virginia Medical Journal,* 90, 472–474.

Luk, S. and Leung, P. (1989) 'Conners' teacher's rating scale – a validity study in Hong Kong.' *Journal of Child Psychopathology and Psychiatry,* 30, 785–794.

Middleton, J. (1989) 'Annotation: Thinking about head injuries in children.' *Journal of Child Psychology and Psychiatry 30,* 663–670.

Phelan, T. (1995) *1-2-3 Magic.* Glen Ellyn, IL: Child Management Inc.

Resnick, R. and McEvoy, K. (1994) *Attention-Deficit Hyperactivity Disorder: Abstracts of the Psychological and Behavioural Literature, 1971–1994.* Washington, DC.

Riggs, P.D. (1998) 'Clinical approach to treatment of ADHD in adolescents with substance use disorders and conduct disorders.' *Journal of the American Academy of Child Psychiatry 37,* 3, 331–332.

Rosenberg, D., Holttum, J., Gershon, S. (1994) *Textbook of Pharmacotherapy for Child and Adolescent Psychiatric Disorders.* New York: Brunner/Mazel.

Rutter, M. (1967) 'A children's behaviour questionnaire for completion by teachers: Preliminary findings.' *Journal of Child Psychology and Psychiatry 8,* 1–11.

Rutter, M., Chadwick, O. and Schaffer, D. (1983) 'Head injury.' In M. Rutter (ed) *Developmental Neuropsychiatry.* Edinburgh: Churchill Livingstone.

Rutter, M., Graham, P. and Yule, W. (1970) 'A neuropsychiatric study of childhood.' *Clinics in Developmental Medicine 101/102.* Oxford: Blackwell Scientific Publications.

Rutter, M., Taylor, E., and Hersov, L. (1994) *Child and Adolescent Psychiatry, Modern Approaches.* Oxford: Blackwell Science Ltd.

Sattersfield, J.H., and Schell, A. (1997) 'A prospective study of Hyperactive boys with conduct problems and normal boys: adolescent and adult criminality.' *Journal of the American Academy of Child and Adolescent Psychiatry, 36,* 12, 1726–1735.

Shekim, W., Kashami, J., Beck, N., Cantwell, D., Martin, J., Rosenberg, J. and Costello, A. (1985) 'The prevalence of attention deficit disorders in a rural midwestern community sample of nine-year-old children.' *Journal of the American Academy of Child Psychiatry 24,* 765–770.

Shen, Y., and Wang, Y. (1984) 'Urinary3-methoxy-4-hydroxy-phenyl-glycoll sulfate excretion in seventy-three school children with minimal brain dysfunction syndrome.' *Biological Psychiatry,* 19, 861–877.

Skuse, D. (1989) 'Psychosocial adversity and impaired growth: In search of causal mechanisms.' In G. Wilkinson (ed) *The Scope of Epidemiological Psychiatry: Essays in Honour of Michael Shepherd.* London: Routledge.

Spencer, T., Biederman, J., Wilens, T., Harding, M., O'Donnell, D., and Griffin, S. (1996) 'Pharmacotherapy of attention-deficit hyperactivity disorder across the life cycle.' *Journal of the American Academy of Child and Adolescent Psychiatry 35,* 4, 407–432.

Stores, G. (1978) 'School children with epilepsy at risk for learning and behavior problems.' *Developmental Medicine and Child Neurology 20,* 502–508.

Szatmari, P., Offord, D.R., and Boyle, M.H. (1989) 'Ontario child health study: Prevalence of attention deficit disorder with hyperactivity.' *Journal of Child Psychology and Psychiatry,* 30, 219–230.

Taylor, E., Schachar, R., Thorley, G., and Wieselberg, M. (1986) 'Conduct disorder and hyperactivity.' *British Journal of Psychiatry,* 12, 143–156.

Taylor, E., Sandberg, S., Thorley, G., and Giles, S. (1991) *The Epidemiology of Childhood Hyperactivity, Maudsley Monographs, 33.* Oxford: Oxford University Press.

Weiss, G. and Hechtman, L.T. (1986) *Hyperactivity Children Grown Up.* New York: Guilford Press.

Wender, P., Epstein, R., Kopin, I. and Gordon, E. (1971) 'Urinary monoamino metabocites in children with minimal brain dysfunction.' *American Journal of Psychiatry 127,* 1411–1415.

Wilens, T., Biederman, J., Spencer, T., and Prince, J. (1995) 'Pharmacotherapy of adult attention deficit/hyperactivity disorder: A Review.' *Journal of Clinical Psychopharmacology 15,* 4, 270–279.

World Health Organization (1992) *The ICD-10 Classification of Mental and Behavioural Disorders. Clinical Descriptions and Diagnostic Guidelines.* Geneva: WHO.

Subject Index

Author Index